Penguin Books
The House of Hospitalities

Emma Tennant was born in London and grew up in the borders of Scotland. Her first novel, *The Colour of Rain*, was published in 1963 under the pseudonym Catherine Aydy and was reissued under her name in 1988. In 1975 Emma Tennant founded and edited the literary newspaper *Bananas*. Her other novels include *Hotel de Dream*, *Bad Sister*, *Woman Beware Woman*, *The Adventures of Robina* and *A Wedding of Cousins*. She is general editor of Penguin Lives of Modern Women series and lives in West London. She has a son and two daughters.

The House of Hospitalities (Viking 1987) is the first volume in Emma Tennant's new 'Cycle of the Sun' series. The second volume, *A Wedding of Cousins*, has recently been published by Viking. Emma Tennant is currently working on the third volume, *The Christening Party*.

The House of Hospitalities

Emma Tennant

PENGUIN BOOKS

PENGUIN BOOKS

Published by the Penguin Group
27 Wrights Lane, London W8 5TZ, England
Viking Penguin Inc., 40 West 23rd Street, New York, New York 10010, USA
Penguin Books Australia Ltd, Ringwood, Victoria, Australia
Penguin Books Canada Ltd, 2801 John Street, Markham, Ontario, Canada L3R 1B4
Penguin Books (NZ) Ltd, 182–190 Wairau Road, Auckland 10, New Zealand

Penguin Books Ltd, Registered Offices: Harmondsworth, Middlesex, England

First published by Viking 1987
Published in Penguin Books 1988

10 9 8 7 6 5 4 3 2 1

Reproduced, printed and bound in Great Britain by
Hazell Watson & Viney Limited
Member of BPCC plc
Aylesbury, Bucks, England
Filmset in Palatino

'Some say that we are different people at different periods of our lives, changing not through effort of will, which is a brave affair, but in the easy course of nature every ten years or so . . . I don't hold with it; I think one remains the same person throughout, merely passing, as it were, in these lapses of time from one room to another, but all in the same house.'

J. M. Barrie, from 'To the Five'

CHAPTER ONE

We left the top of the downs and came down into the Lovegrove Valley. Every inch, I thought, of this country has been used and then used again. There are no secrets here: where there are ridges there are Roman soldiers, knees blue in the cold of a Wiltshire dawn; under the ancient yews men reach to cut wood for their bows; that grass bowl, with the stone house lopsided against it, was a parliament once, where Saxons sat like spectators in an amphitheatre, pondering the future of their land. Even the nineteenth-century red-brick houses, built for workers in the age of progress, stood like the open pages of a history book: Enlightenment, Paternalism. As we lost height, the downs made a green rule against the sky. The burial mounds of chieftains were gentle punctuation marks along the horizon: it was growing dark. The countryside was as familiar and comforting as a childhood blanket, worn in places, with holes of blackness where the night fell in a combe or dip. Nothing would surprise me here: I knew it all even though I had never been before.

Amy must have sensed what I was thinking. She knew something, too, of the hard time I'd had getting permission to come to Lovegrove. 'We don't know anything about them,' my Aunt Babs had said, standing in an unusual (for her) arms akimbo position in the sitting-room of our North Kensington home. 'You mightn't like it there, Jenny. And what are you going to take to wear?' But Amy was speaking now, against the receding memory of Aunt Babs' worried voice; and I smiled out at the dusk, the shadows under the elms, as we plunged on down the steep hills in the black Bentley that had been at Salisbury Station to meet us. What I had been warned against was already proved wrong. I would feel strange, Aunt Babs said. I wasn't used to it. 'My grandmother used to go up to Stonehenge in her caravan, with horses,' Amy said. 'We can go there tomorrow.' And, as if she had picked up my pleasure, my odd feeling of homecoming, she said, 'You understand it here, Jenny, don't you? I can feel it.' And she gave my arm a squeeze.

If all this sounds mystical – fanciful, at least – I dare say it's because fourteen-year-old schoolchildren are hardly aware of the origins of their sensations (and even less of the complicated and sometimes still childish motivations of their elders). I had no idea then, for instance, that Aunt Babs' Sunday School feelings of what was 'right' and what was wrong would bias her automatically against Amy's parents. This may appear naîve but is the simple truth: for Aunt Babs was a Labour voter – and she was caring for me while my parents were posted abroad – coming to the School Jumble Sale, talking to everyone as if they were exactly the same.

But when it came to the Lovescombes, a hard, rather distant look came into her eyes. 'I read somewhere that they've moved back into Lovegrove,' she said, 'after spending the war in a house in the village.' And she gave a dry laugh. 'Go if you really must, Jenny.' Her voice dropped, as if she had no wish to be overheard; as if, despite the fact we were alone in her thin 'through room' that looked out the back on the mews where the vegetable sellers from

Portobello market kept their wheeled, wooden stalls (departing every morning like a succession of sedan chairs to their sites) – as if one of these proletarian and much-lauded figures were about to climb up onto the window-sill and hear her mention the privileged folk with whom her niece was going to stay. 'But if they change in the evening,' added Aunt Babs, menacingly, 'you'll just have to explain that you haven't got anything to wear.' Another pause, while I contemplated myself at supper, as in a nightmare, in nothing but my underclothes. 'And don't forget to tip the maid.'

I must say, too, that this feeling of happy return on arrival in the Lovegrove Valley was probably a sentimental one. Landscapes and people become inextricably mixed where the emotions are concerned: I hardly knew then if I was half in love with Amy or on the edge of a new love which lay, like the valley so-named, in the darkness ahead: all I knew, after the drab months of a London summer, still threadbare after the war, was that I wanted magic, which the old clock of Stonehenge puts about on nights such as these: greensward, rooks-flying-from-the-high-wood and all.

'Here we are,' Amy said, as we turned by the squat shoulder of a Norman church and down a drive with edges bursting with cow-parsley, ragged robin and speedwell in a blue haze in the grass. 'I'm so glad there's just a little light left, so we can explore.' And, seeing my surprise: 'I still explore here every holidays. Didn't I tell you, I found a little round house with a thatched roof in the wood. My grandmother built it for the children, they used to sleep there. And there was a *moat* round it!' Then, for she must have seen a very different expression on my face, she fell silent for a moment. The Bentley crunched on gravel, the drive having ended in a great circle of grass: to the far side of us was the stable block which, once we were gone, would swallow the car up for the night. I opened the door and climbed out. Lovegrove was in front of me – all round me, rather, and involuntarily I stepped back against the car. Amy walked – I had never seen her walk like that, I thought, with a sort of stiff keenness – towards the front steps and, turning, beckoned for me to come. 'Well, Jenny? Look, we can go on the river if we're quick!'

I followed Amy up the steps and to the edge of the hall. The driver was ahead of me now, Amy's suitcase in one hand and my cardboard case, subject of much rummaging and sighing on the part of Aunt Babs (who never went anywhere, and said London in August was the best season of the year), in the other. My heart was sinking fast. Where was the feeling of familiarity now? The downs were still there, in a line of dark blue-green against a sky that seemed to have settled into a permanent half-night. Elms and chestnuts stood as recognizably and firmly as before. Church and churchyard, in the uncertain distance, looked as reassuring as a set of nursery bricks, to be picked up, played with and reassembled at will. But I no longer felt at home. I had never seen or imagined anywhere like Lovegrove Manor in my life.

It's said that the rich are different because they're richer. But there must also be some tone, some aura invisible to all except each other, perhaps, and those eager to join them: one of those auras of colour, purplish or blue, such as were seen in spiritualist 'photographs' at the time of the First War. As with the humours of former times, these auras showed a disposition melancholy, avaricious, saturnine; so also there must be some way of declaring the halo of earthly gold other than in balance sheets, profit and loss. Amy was a case in point. For in a school with three hundred and upward girls (and all in the hideous uniform of St Peter's in that day, which was, I suppose, 1953) she stood out absolutely. In a sea of blue-and-white ruled blouses, under a gym slip of barbaric cut, she shone like some distant, pale star – fallen among us, but not to stay for long. Different. Rich.

If all this sounds impossibly subjective (certainly there was no place for this way of perceiving things in Aunt Babs' philosophy: Nurture not Nature produced the end result, the Child was but a poor shadow of the Man), then how to account for Amy standing out in this undeniable way? She wasn't known for any special gift or talent – she was un-musical to the extent, if I remember, that she couldn't keep in tune in the school hymn-singing and stayed silent. She wasn't hard-working (well, why should she be? She had no living ahead of her to gain); she wasn't so beautiful, as some people are, that eyes won't keep off them, that the whole mystery of what is beauty, proportion, divine allo-cation of feature comes into play. She acted in school drama, but not particularly well – causing the English teacher, the day after a halting performance, to stop Amy in the gallery and compliment her on her legs. So what was it that she had – or was 'it' just the reflected awe and snobbery of hundreds of other, lesser stars, that made her stand out in the way she did? Was she proof that England, after a long and bitter struggle, was still torn by Class War? And did Amy represent the love/hate for that pernicious system, handed down from parents to their children, chil-dren all of ambitious parents, most middle-class, some objects of patronage (for St Peter's, West London was a Direct-Grant School as such institutions were then known, meaning that to achieve some semblance of equality free places were dished out to a number of the 'less advantaged')? I don't know the answer to any of this. All I do know is that half the school was in love with Amy – and especially after her performance as Hamlet when, in an age that preceded tights – when as girls at school we wore white ankle socks and at home nylons and painful 'roll-ons' with suspenders, Amy's legs in black tights caused a sensation. Little wonder, perhaps, that the English teacher, in a school that was intellectually formidable, hardly known for its frivolities in the way of appearance and clothing, paused in the upper gallery to make comment.

But that isn't enough. Amy, it was true, had an attractive page-boy look: her short hair swung in a curved blade, the same length all the way round, like a youth in a medieval tapestry; there was a vaguely unsettled air about her, too, which suggested she might step out of the tapestry at any moment and slay the dragon herself. The androgynous air conquered the uniform, the 'sash' of white cord which cut the body in half and left most of its wearers no more than a bundle of potatoes. It was the legs that did it, I suppose: they were so long and slender that they looked, sometimes, as if they might snap. Her body seemed no more than dashed in, between legs like these and a long neck, with the pensive face atop: Joan of Arc when she sat at her easel in the art class, looking up; suddenly clumsy if asked to perform some favour, or menial deed (she never did at home, no doubt); but clumsy in the way of a Shakespearian lad, a Tom or Dick, fresh-faced and laughing, staggering with logs into the Hall.

It was in fact at art class that this mysterious, subtle 'difference' most plainly showed itself to me. Like most girls in their first term (I'd come late to St Peter's, having been to school outside London, in Hertfordshire, where I lived with my parents until my father's posting to a minor Civil Service job in Barbados), I was more concerned with finding my way about, and making my way too through the difficult and demanding work, than in noticing very much about any girl not in my immediate vicinity. Amy was in the same class – but she sat right at the back (I only discovered later how myopic she was, she just saw the blackboard through a haze, I suppose, and didn't give a damn about it) – and my whole attention, when not studying or walking/not-running in the long corridors and galleries of St Peter's, was taken up by the girl at the next desk to mine: a girl who was for her part entirely taken up with her desire to be with Amy. Her name was Candida Tarn.

There's probably a very simple reason why the art class was the place where personalities emerged. The 'sameness' among pupils encouraged by St Peter's was – especially in that oasis of time 'Double Art' – overlaid by eccentricities, foibles, sudden bursts of loud talking even, which would never have been possible in the long, arduous lessons intended to prepare us for a life that was professional and probably celibate. The reason lies doubtless in the liberating effect of splashing paint on paper (we were 'doing' Turner that term). And in this case, the art teacher, a woman who seemed to stand for all that the school did not, must certainly have been a spur to the feeling of freedom and excitement that started up as soon as one climbed the stairs to the long studio art-room at the top of the Victorian house that was St Peter's, West London.

Miss Carston was known slightly to my Aunt Babs. Behind both women perhaps lay the same struggle – for independence, for recognition of artistic talents (my Aunt Babs had taught in an infant school in Camden Town and now painted at home when she had the time from organizing her stall). But the difference between them, to put it brutally, was that Miss Carston had a famous artist as a brother, which secured her a place teaching at St Peter's (and also a magisterial air, like a ship in a smock, sailing along the wide seas of the art-room), while my aunt, coming from a 'dull' military family, had no one to help or lend a famous name. It was obvious too that Miss Carston, like my aunt, had made no overt decision to remain unmarried: it had just happened to them that they stayed alone. But whereas Aunt Babs had gently pushed away the unsuitable admirers (in her eyes at least) who wanted, or so she said, free meals for life, Miss Carston gave off so strong and repelling an impression of actually being married already – to her distinguished brother, to her 'art' – that no one could have imagined a suitor brave enough to propose. It was in the context of this brother – Sidney Carston – that Miss Carston saw life, and whether or not his own art was relevant to whatever Miss Carston was teaching, she would bring it up relentlessly, causing bafflement sometimes in the class when El Greco, say, was forcibly compared to the artist Sidney Carston. It was, however, just possible to think of Sidney Carston and J. M. W. Turner together, at least when it came to representations of the weather; and Miss Carston was reminding us, on that day when Amy's 'specialness' became clear to me for the first time, that her brother liked to 'wash in' water scenes with his fingers – this possibly being a trick of Turner's as well. Miss Carston stopped dramatically by my easel, stuck her finger in my painting-water and made a great swirl of inky grey-blue on my paper. 'Sidney' (for so she liked to call the great man when she was in a good mood, if she was angry he was 'Mr Carston RA') – 'Sidney believes in freedom of movement. He would never let this sort of thing' – and here Miss Carston pulled a sheet from the desk of Candida Tarn – 'he would expel this painter from the Slade!'

All of us were used to these incomprehensible statements, and today Miss Carston seemed only mildly eccentric as we were, after all, supposed to be copying a Turner watercolour of the Thames at Whitehall Stairs and, for all we knew, Sidney Carston had often depicted the very same subject.

I looked down at my ruined paper and was about to take it off the easel when Miss ,Carston ripped it off for me and held it triumphantly aloft. 'Here we see the real thing,' she proclaimed. 'Water, life, movement, Art.'

I have never liked being the centre of attention – as we shall see it didn't last for long that Miss Carston stood waving her own smudge as proof of the magic, free way – and I felt sorry too for Candida Tarn, a quiet girl who had, it seemed from Miss Carston's demonstration of her attempt at a water-scene, been only too neat in its execution. 'Who says that we have the right to tell water where to go?' exclaimed Miss Carston. 'Sidney has never given instructions to water. Canaletto, the great Canaletto, was obedient to the dictates of water. But Candida here, Candida Tarn, has set the river flowing away from the sea, up, up, to the hills from whence it came. Candida, isn't this rather God-like on your part?'

It was hard to see, from the aqueous offering held out, whether Candida's intention to send the river back, so to speak, whence it came wasn't a kinder one than the messy whirlpool which my own inexpertise and Miss Carston's finger had jointly produced. Candida's brush-strokes, regular and well-spaced, suggested a need to brush the whole inconvenient wetness out of the way. Miss Carston's scorn, however, was clearly unmitigated by any such consideration. As if to punish Candida, who, I'd noticed in ordinary lessons, went very white when criticized and lowered her head, not in humility, it seemed, but as if preparing to butt her attacker, Miss Carston dashed the paper from the easel next door and called for silence, a certain amount of giggling having broken out. 'If I look at the standard of waterscapes painted here this morning' – and here she broke off, plunged her finger in a pot of black paint, and, aerially, as it were, added a small black craft, a dug-out possibly, or a canoe, to 'my' picture – 'I have only to look at samples, taken at random, to prove my point, which is that last week's lesson went unheeded – hands up who can remember it? The name of the painting of the Avon at Amesbury by Sidney Carston RA, which we studied in detail – yes, yes, I thought so, we don't have any show of hands from Candida Tarn . . . Now, Miss Tarn, if you wish to sleep in the Art lesson you must have a letter from your mother requesting permission. And in English if you please!'

Before there was time to register yet another instance of Miss Carston's intense dislike of anything 'unEnglish' (Candida's family, being German refugees, certainly would have no part in the landscape, or indeed the weather depicted by Sidney Carston RA) there came the sound – a sound and then a succession of sounds so loud, careless, arrogant even, that Miss Carston was forced to lower her watercolour – sounds which were the first intimation, as I have said, of an unconscious superiority assumed, and agreed with, for the most part, by staff and other pupils alike.

Candida Tarn, glad to free herself from my company, I dare say, and particularly glad to be able to place herself next to Amy, had done just that: their easels were adjacent, even touching, and Candida had pulled her chair as near to her idol's as she could (though Miss Carston, as unaware as Queen Victoria of Sapphic love, would hardly have remonstrated if Candida had lain prone at Amy's feet, thinking probably that the girl was posing for some classical subject, Demeter and Persephone perhaps, and was practising lowering herself into the earth, through wild flowers, as described by John Milton and painted by Sidney Carston RA). As it was, the sounds – which were sneezes – were instantly attributed to Candida rather than her neighbour. Miss Carston wheeled round sharply. A silence fell. The sneezes, like the first declaration of Revolution, had had total abandon: a sort of suicide mission of sneezes, as if their progenitor was looking only for a way to be expelled from the mortal coils of St Peter's and find a new life outside. 'Candida! Stand up!' said Miss Carston. 'But Miss Carston . . .' said Candida.

It would be tedious here to outline one of those 'incidents' so common in schools where an authoritarian regime clashes regularly with rebellious girls – except for the fact that there were very few rebellious girls in those days, when 'dropping out' had never even been dreamt of. There were always one or two real criminals, it's true, and it was possible for every one of us except Miss Carston to guess who had started up this sneezing business.

Carmen Bye was sitting directly behind Amy and Candida. In light of what happened next it was possible to see the roles allotted to the participants in the drama as if these had been written out for them at birth and they were destined to act them in perpetuity: Candida the suspect, Amy the casual passerby with impeccable connections, Carmen the plotter, manipulator, overthrower of regimes. So one might have thought then, at least; and if I am to count myself in as the observer and recorder of these allotted roles I must add that there were to be many variations on this theme, and that not all the startling ones came from the most obvious quarter, which would then, I suppose, have been Carmen.

It's hard to describe Carmen Bye without overdoing the make-up, plastering it on even, so that doubts begin to arise as to the reality of the person underneath. This was because she did so much to add 'colour' herself, and if all the colours sometimes added up to a clown's face, they drew attention and admiration as well as laughter. You never heard contempt for Carmen. She was too aggressive, she might 'say anything', which in an age of intense social and physical embarrassment was to be avoided at all costs. (She had, for a dare, gone up to the Head Girl and asked her if she wanted to buy a cheap sanitary towel.) Carmen's actual appearance, too, lent itself to melodrama of the roughest kind. Long black hair, black eyes, a high-ridged nose and cheekbones that seemed to have been hurled into her face like javelins (this comment on Carmen being made by Bernard Ehrlich, the painter, who was to paint her so often: body a bunch of twisted meat, hair, nose and eyes meeting in an imperious battle across a face that was cadaver-white): all these contributed to an easy belief that Carmen's tales of her origins were true, however often the king-in-exile changed his country or the gypsy mother's violent death changed its way. What *was* known, which was clearly disappointingly prosaic, was that Carmen lived with 'relatives' in Wimbledon. But, unlike the general acceptance of, say, my Aunt Babs, with her visits to School Bazaars and Concerts, Carmen's 'relatives' never came to St Peter's; and nor were any of Carmen's friends, if her slaves and victims can be so described, invited home. Carmen's mystery was an essential ingredient of her character.

The sneezing powder dropped down Amy's blouse from behind by Carmen eventually came to light, but not before Candida had been sent to stand in the corridor outside the art-room; and nor was she immediately called in when the error was finally discovered. It was through this incident that I saw, and didn't want to see, something about the unfairness of life – I suppose I had been sheltered by my parents and then by the eminently 'fair' Aunt Babs – and I must confess that for a time, 'unfair' though it undoubtedly was, I turned against Amy, deciding to be the only person in this great school who was actually not in love with her.

Miss Carston started off well enough. 'It takes two,' she announced, Candida having been despatched and the other girls settling down, after the great expression of disdain that had been the sneezes. 'Carmen, you will report to the Head for having this powder. Amy, you could surely have controlled yourself?'

Amy, who was sitting slouched in her chair, with her long legs out in front at an unnatural angle, suggesting more disdain somehow, as if she were more interested in arranging her limbs to look like an architect's compasses, or a Cubist pattern as far removed as possible from the work of Sidney Carston RA, looked up briefly at the suggestion of greater self-control. Her page-boy hair swung round her face, which she dipped down so that her eyes looked very wide up at Miss Carston. She settled even deeper in her chair, so that the long body and slender legs looked even more like those of a boy who has been sent away from home – the son of a noble family sent to serve another. A sigh from an admirer sounded from the back of the room. The feeling, supposedly banished from Britain, that you can't punish the rich and well-born suggested itself strongly. Miss Carston's face took on a distant expression – as if to put all this childish nonsense behind her – and, addressing the scion of the great family as the inheritor one day of fine things (which at once put Amy in an ageless category, money and possessions, like the Crown, conferring an immediate authority), said, 'By the way, Amy, I read somewhere that Lovegrove is going to open to the public. I was interested to see that they have been building up a collection of modern art. Do you know if that particular room will be among those on public view?'

Amy simply slumped further in her chair. It was possible to feel the incredulity of the others in the art-room at this extraordinary casualness. There was a silence. We were all uncomfortable, I think: Miss Carston was 'potty', as we liked to agree, but to see her humiliated and exposed as a snob would be somehow painful. 'If so,' Miss Carston went on bravely, 'do please tell your parents I'd be only too happy to help them build up the collection further. Ensuring a fine representation of contemporary artists . . .'

A girl at the back scraped her chair and stood up. The lesson had run over already and we were late, too late, thankfully, to hear Miss Carston plead for the inclusion of a Sidney Carston RA at Amy's parents' home. We trooped out. Amy, who had only shrugged at Miss Carston's question – showing ignorance? indifference? – sauntered out behind us. Miss Carston pounced on Candida, still lingering in the corridor. 'Candida, clear up this mess.' Resuming authority, she pushed Candida, whose pale, stubborn face was lowered still, goat-like: 'Mop it up!' The 'mess' consisted of the watercolour to which Miss Carston had added her Turner-esque appearance; an old handkerchief on the floor, left over from the sneezes, and sweet papers round and underneath Amy and Carmen's chairs. Candida went down on hands and knees and scooped the 'mess' into a waste-paper basket.

'And hurry up about it,' Miss Carston said. 'Anyone would think you had all day, Candida Tarn.'

CHAPTER TWO

To say what it was that brought me, within six weeks of this scene, to an evening drive through a landscape that had for many years known the touch and tutelage of the Lovescombe family – fences neatly kept, fresh thatching on the farm cottages by the side of the road, modern milking sheds and the gleam of new machinery – would be to go further than I can now in the account of Amy at school; of Candida's way of making up to Amy and the strain of her obsession, which was felt by all; of the invitation to Lovegrove, which Candida had prayed for nightly. Now, as a culmination to the 'crush' Candida had developed and Amy's embarrassed, nonchalant acceptance of it, an outbreak of chicken-pox had brought Candida to her bed and me to Lovegrove instead of her.

Why did I go? That would be hard, too, to explain. Had Amy seen, as the very sought-after will sometimes do, my slight drawing-back from her and wooed me, almost, so that I had no choice but to capitulate? Perhaps. Yet I must say too that I wanted to see this world of which even Miss Carston spoke with awe: I dreamt less and less of Hertfordshire, which my parents had let while they were abroad, and I had little desire to spend the summer in London with Aunt Babs, who made wherever she was a curious and rather messy amalgam of urban and rural life, cultivating a garden of wild-flowers and weeds where dropped bus tickets blew in from the noisy street beyond and the London cats hid and hissed. I wanted to see everything I imagined to lie in the name Lovegrove; and to my childish mind this was a great bowl, Chinese porcelain probably (for Aunt Babs had pointed one out to me in the V & A and said the rich eighteenth-century English had liked to order their designs made up for them in China), a great bowl, exquisitely drawn all round with scenes from the Lovescombe lives: birds in dovecotes, riding, fields of barley and of rye – everything, in short, that a romantic education in English and a need for love (which is really the need to satisfy an overwhelming curiosity) could bring to a young person after years spent as a lonely evacuee in Canada in the War, followed by a dull house outside St Albans, the red-brick walls, flat fields, cars and cows. I saw too, or rather smelt, a pot pourri that lay in this bowl, all roses and lavender and peonies gathered in the gardens at Lovegrove. Roses that climbed, made arches, spread in great bushes onto the lawns.

I was ready for all of this. But I was in no way ready for the reality of the place, though the smell of hundreds of summers was indeed there in the hall. A Chinese bowl was on the chest as you walked in, a plate lay beside it – for letters both outgoing and newly arrived, as I was to learn – a bowl filled with the heady mix of petal and herb, but with dragons round the sides and the gold and scarlet roof of a pagoda guarding the lavender mixture. Fishing rods stood either side of the chest, and there was a flight of marble stairs up to a landing and a door – which had swung shut after Amy – and on the walls pictures of game, eyes as bright in death as their plumes, which were Chinese too: for the pheasant, like the priceless porcelain from the East, was brought over for the amusement and pleasure of the English rich. There were hares too, painted dead and laid out in a 'bag', as I was to hear a day of this slaughter called. A stuffed salmon, plump, faded as a dowager at one of the long-forgotten Lovegrove 'balls', was framed on the wall at the top of the stairs.

If all around was dead, it was hardly surprising, among this almost Egyptian exhibition of the taxidermist's art, that the butler descending the marble flight of steps seemed at first to be stuffed also. Vertical on the white slab of the stairs and against the gloom of the hall he certainly 'belonged': even his eye had a cold look, like the salmon in all its finery of reed and frond on the far wall. He approached, though; and I shrank back, wanting Amy. What was 'one' supposed to do? Aunt Babs, grimly packing a 'tip for the staff' in an envelope among my summer dresses, had hardly envisaged this.

'Good evening, Miss,' said this black-suited, cold and sharp-eyed man. He was tall and bulky: I backed away from him and went to the Chinese bowl on the chest, nervously dipping my finger, as a young child might, in floral remains that crumbled to dust under my touch. 'Will your maid be arriving on the later train?' asked the butler. And he glanced down at my case, Aunt Babs' poor case, and then away again.

I don't know, if Amy hadn't reappeared, how this particular scene would have ended – for I felt on the one hand that I must abandon the case, flee down the drive, take shelter first in the squat church and then creep in the direction of home as it grew dark and the shadows from the tall oaks came across the road with their festoons of smaller ivy shadows; and on the other that in this plethora of shade and obscurity I might lose myself altogether.

The full unknown-ness of the country came home to me.

I might have felt a sense, on the drive, of cosy familiarity with the landscape – the well-placed trees to keep out the wind, the streams with bridges every mile or so into fields of buttercups and flag iris, the tops of the copper beeches like red birds' nests – but what of the night, and the throttling dark, worse than the black knots of ivy that swung to dance on the face, all unseen? No bus, anywhere. And it certainly was growing dark, both outside and increasingly in the dim hall, where the black shape of the butler drew nearer and seemed to ask again about the anticipated arrival of my own personal domestic.

'Don't be silly, Vine, of course Jenny hasn't got a maid.' To my vast relief Amy's voice sounded through the now open door into the main hall. From here there was a glimpse of grass-green carpet, white pillars, giant fuchsias and lilies: like heaven, it seemed to me, after the mortuary of the outer hall, with its grim attendant. Vine, as this apparition was apparently known, took the news of my maidlessness less hard than I had feared from his initial tone, and proceeded to turn, showing I was to follow him and be escorted, ferried, as it were, across the Styx, but in the opposite direction to the normal one, going in this case from the land of the dead to the living. Charon (as I was always to think of him after this first encounter with the inheritance of the plutocratic English: the painstaking pictorial representation of dead flesh) now steered me, as if I were in fact a bark without the power to go along the landing alone, to the door of the main hall which Amy, still laughing, held open. 'Whatever happened to you, Jenny?' she said. 'Come and say hello to everyone and then let's run outside while there's still light.'

CHAPTER THREE

'Saying hello to everyone' turned out to be a harder, even more baffling process than I could have imagined. For one thing, who was 'everyone'? Did they include Miss Bolt – 'Oh Boltie, this is Jenny,' Amy said, as I flew after her down the length of the grass-green hall and in and out of pillars which in turn appeared to hold up stairs and landings and more flights of stairs again, as if the entire house were based on architectural fantasy or a dream. But who was 'Boltie'? Sewing-basket and a sheaf of papers in hand, she was clearly a governess or housekeeper: but if she was a governess, then why did Amy go to school? To get used to ordinary people, I had to think. Shut up here she'd never be able to cope with the outside world. Was 'Boltie' herself employed to represent ordinary people? So that, in this almost Moorish arrangement of exotic flowers, internal courtyard, long lawns and avenues of trees going up to downs where only the lark, in those days, made a sound in a wide blue sky entirely the property of Lord Lovescombe, the inhabitants of Lovegrove could look to a plain little woman 'with her feet on the ground' for stability and reassurance? Or, if you grew up here and believed it to be run-of-the-mill, did the outside world seem impossibly mean, full of 'Bolties' and hardly worth living in? What happened, exactly, to those born like Amy with a silver spoon as long as your arm and crested, too, wedged firmly in their jaws?

These thoughts, more pertinent than I could then have known, were further provoked, when we slowed down at the far end of the majestic hall, by the portraits, separated by shelves of books in rich leather and by doors of a light wood, gold-handled; portraits, I couldn't help supposing, of some of the present occupants of the place? They were put about so naturally, somehow, their faces, glowing and ruddy, looking as if they had just been painted, and the odd wig or lace ruffling seeming no more than a slight affectation. They were alive, certainly, unlike the parlour of dead game which was the first sight of Lovegrove; and their witty, intelligent expressions seemed benevolent, even mildly curious, as Amy and I dawdled to a slower walk. 'Here we are,' Amy said, throwing open the light-grained door on the right of a velvet-coated man, more pompous than the rest, heavy with jowls and a rotten borough to his name, 'I think Mummy's bound to be in here.'

I hadn't been far off the mark either, it seemed, when it came to a strong resemblance between the portraits and the actual occupants of the house; this resemblance coming not so much from inherited features as from an expression of enjoyment and simple repose. The faces in real life in the sitting-room (or drorring-room, as Amy called it) were so full of the space and beauty of the surroundings that they had regressed in type to the eighteenth century. This impression was all the stronger for Lady Lovescombe's white curls, a 'Pompadour', that was threaded with blue ribbon, and the other woman's silk dress, mutton-chop sleeves and all, that suggested she had just come in from milking the goats at the Petit Trianon. 'Mummy,' Amy said to the white-haired one (the other, who turned out to be

Lord Lovescombe's sister, Amalia Drifton, was black-haired, slightly haggard, but still with that mysterious air of proprietorship and ease), 'Mummy, this is Jenny. Jenny Carter.'

If I had come from the moon I couldn't have been given a more casual and polite greeting; the distance implied in Lady Lovescombe's slight touch of the hand, and in her leaning forward on the enormous sofa (which would in itself take up the whole of Aunt Babs' 'through room', I calculated, leaving no room for the console tables either side, with their tall vases of delphinium, Albertine rose, peonies and poppies as large and red as rumpled heads) implying that the further forward she leaned, the further away from each other Lady Lovescombe and I would be. She had searched my face in the first few seconds for traces of 'family' and had found them missing – I didn't know this then, of course, but I could feel the chill of no interest, of a friend of Amy's, brought from the school where she was sent precisely to make such friends, and very boring they turned out to be too. 'And Aunt Amalia,' Amy said.

In some ways I liked Amalia Drifton better than Amy's mother. She made no pretence, at least, of regarding me in a hopeful and ethereal way, as if my superior qualities, not immediately discernible, would come through soon and confirm Amy's rightness of choice in selecting me for the honour of a place at Lovegrove. Amalia Drifton simply went on talking, as if we were no more than ghostly visitors. I stood in my most awkward position, copied, I suppose, from a father in the civil service who was in turn copying the stance of the consort of our new Queen: hands clasped behind back and feet apart. Amy had wandered to a desk under a far window, where she appeared to be turning the pages of a gargantuan blank book, bound in tortoiseshell and calf.

'I simply can't see the point,' Amalia Drifton went on, to Lady Lovescombe. 'I mean, the Hares have so terribly *little* money! Why buy a *bigger* house just when their only son grows up and goes to Oxford?'

'I can't imagine,' said Lady Lovescombe, the faintest tinge of impatience in her voice. 'They don't entertain.'

'I've heard that Jack Hare is now completely dotty,' Amalia Drifton insisted. 'I mean, poor Loelia. And they used to go out all the time – and try to give dinners in their *tiny* house –'

'Space is important, though,' Lady Lovescombe said. Her dying-sigh voice carried surprisingly round the drawing-room.

'I know. But to do nothing in? I mean, Jasmine told me Loelia hasn't got enough *furniture* for this new house. And no money to buy any, either.'

'Furniture has become so terribly expensive,' concurred Lady Lovescombe.

'But Jasmine says that they're so desperately unhappy together,' insisted Amalia Drifton, skipping, as it were, the furniture. 'Jasmine says Loelia would do *anything* to get away. Those long evenings getting drunk with Arthur Koestler, and d'you know they're both sick very often . . . isn't it disgusting?'

'Who? Jasmine and Loelia?' said Lady Lovescombe, with a shade of satisfaction this time to be discerned.

'No, *no*,' Amalia was saying as I moved, for the need of something to do, closer to Amy and the gigantic book which she was now stooping low over, as if about to trap an insect in its pages, 'No, *no*, Jack and Arthur Koestler, or whatever he's called. Sick on those little bits of Aubusson that Loelia has on the boards . . .'

'Jasmine Tremlett,' Amy suddenly read out from the

pages of the book, 'I thought she was staying here now, Mummy. Not last week.'

I thought for a moment how Lovegrove must be like a garrison, or a small township, where the number of people coming in and out fluctuates, and some sort of record is kept for the sake of supplies.

'It would be worse if she had a big carpet,' said Lady Lovescombe, still thinking of the grisly evenings at the Hares, no doubt. I wondered if I would meet people like this, and, in my mind's eye, saw the type of cartoon, much enjoyed by my father's father and his family, of eighteenth-century noblemen spewing out the contents of their stomachs in reply to an innocent remark from a bystander. If the light and beauty of that age had manifested itself with these privileged people, so perhaps had the unpleasant habits, such as being sick all over the place. Less surprise at Aunt Babs' initial reluctance to let me go to stay with these 'people we don't know anything about' followed. Conceivably she knew only too much of their way of going on.

Amy, however, was making her point about dates in the visitors' book with renewed effort – despite Lady Loves-combe's cool, slightly too uninterested air, and despite also the opening of the french window from the garden and the appearance in the room of a dark, bearded man in a white cable cardigan. He paused a moment as he came in, not expecting to see two girls there, I suppose, not knowing whether he should be introduced.

'She was here last weekend,' Amy said, having peered at the slab of a book, in which guests inscribed their names before going out into the real world of 'austerity', as it came later to be known, the grey world of post-war Britain. I saw them being ferried by Vine, past the glazed eyes of the dead trophies and on to the sweep of the front drive. 'She can't have been, though,' Amy was saying: the first time I had heard her sound shrill, I thought. 'Lovegrove wasn't opened up last weekend. Was it, Mummy?'

The new information that this apparently permanent heaven was in fact closed down at intervals so took me aback that I missed, only to reconstruct much later, the glacial tone in Lady Lovescombe's voice and its reasons. I was aware, certainly, of an uncomfortable current in the room, as if all the doors had opened at once and an ugly, draught-ridden chamber had been revealed, with too many openings into hall, garden and other rooms not yet specified. Lady Lovescombe, however, rose to the occasion and half-turned in the sofa, giving the extraordinary impression of someone who has risen to their feet to greet a guest and then sat down again. The folds of her dress, which was of a white linen coarsely woven with the same bluish thread as she wore in her hair, gave a graceful ripple. So it was at the Court of Prince Genji, doubtless, as recorded by the Lady Murasaki; and my self-conscious realization of this came too from a memory of the disapproval of Aunt Babs when she had found me, Arthur Waley's translation in hand (a book found among my parents' crates of books when they packed up to go abroad) and deep in the world of eleventh-century Japan rather than the world of maths at St Peter's and essays on *Tess* and *Far from the Madding Crowd*. (I was, of course, at Lovegrove in the world for which Hardy's servants and labourers gave their lives and their souls and were sent packing when these services were no longer wanted, a world immeasurably altered by the war, so that only a few as rich as Lord Lovescombe evidently was would 'keep on' such as Vine or Miss Bolt, let alone the other domestics who must exist to prime the pump of Lovegrove. And a world so far from Hardy's preoccupations, too, that he must have seen little of it, for all his first wife's social pretensions.) Yet, since the days he described, at least, there was another difference again. The sheer opulence of the Edwardians had brought a tinge of vulgarity to these echelons of English life. Lady Loves-combe, for all her French marquise rig, was overlaid by this, too, and it was maybe for this reason that I saw her and her world as further than anything I could ever imagine from my own – as far, say, and as foreign as the world of the Shining Prince and his court.

Lady Lovescombe's rippling movement was the start of an introduction process. Amy still stood over by the offend-ing visitors' book, which was closed now on the top of a Chippendale table, a silver inkstand and quill at its side for the next signatory. 'Jim,' said Lady Lovescombe in that featherlight voice which carried with it too the promise of poison, the venom tip to the dart, 'Jim, this is a . . . a friend of Amy's, Jenny . . . Carter. Jenny, this is Jim Tremlett.'

I was saved from the embarrassment of having to stretch out my hand, not knowing if I was meant or expected to do this, by Amy's running over and suddenly putting her arm round my shoulder – something she had never before done – so that we were impossible to meet singly, and like heta-erae supporting a temple column, would have to be seen as a collective thing. 'Amy, how lovely to see you again,' said Jim Tremlett. He paused, decided against the risk of a kiss that would half land on familiar territory and half on strange. 'I think I'll have a bath,' he said, as if to the waiting world, and sauntered to the door. He had an athlete's body slightly gone to seed, I saw – but my eyes, the eyes of youth, were cruel then.

'Come on Jenny,' Amy said, her mother's own gaze still averted from her since the gaffe, or whatever it had been, by the elegant table by the window that looked out on the drive. 'We're going out – but only for one minute,' she said, like a much younger child, to the deflected head, white curls uppermost in a perfect foam. Amalia Drifton, who had been mixing a cocktail (or so I assumed it must be) while all this was going on (or not going on, as I was to discover with so many of the secret correspondences of the Lovescombes), lifted her glass, which looked frozen all over and had a cherry sticking out of the top. 'Silly girls,' she said, but in no tone that suggested anything other than boredom. 'It's almost dark.'

If I had wondered why Amy was so keen to get out of doors that evening at Lovegrove, two steps into the garden supplied the answer. An answer, in fact, so far again from that feeling of 'known-ness' that the landscape on the other side had provided that I hesitated at first to join her – it was too like my dream of the Chinese bowl, too near to the court where whispers and wooden ox-carts carrying the whispering women to each other's screened houses made a rustle from dawn until nightfall; too near that world where poems dropped like courtiers' coloured silks in the sadness of loss, of leaves falling. And it was all close to being invisible. I could pick out the slender bridges, which seemed, in the last of the setting sun, to be painted crimson and gold: gently humped, in a crisscross over innumerable streams, each choked with water-lily pads and wild nasturtiums. I saw the clumps of tall bamboo, but no more than if they had been an army of pale ghosts, a *samurai* revenge on an English garden that had been taken from its roots and twisted, compressed, hidden in loops of water and stone. In the distance, on the far side of the river (the real river, that is, which Amy had told me of, the River Love, a tributary of the Avon), lay water-meadows, willows that appeared to have bowed too to the Chinese fantasy. The sky behind them was pale blue, as in the plates I remembered so well at my father's father's, when willow-pattern was the thing for ginger biscuits, long afternoons in suburbia. Nearer, the sky was a deep blue, so that I could scarcely see Amy as she ran, and hopped the narrow streams and back again, in a complicated game known only to herself. Somewhere in the middle distance, beyond a great cedar half held up by iron girders, was a flat stretch, an artificial stream wider than the rest, spanned by a small house. Amy ran back for me. Her eyes were alive: she seemed to have forgotten the scene with her mother in the drawing-room.

'Amy!' I said. Then I blurted out, 'It's amazing here. I mean . . .'

'My grandmother,' Amy said. She drew me down towards the house on the river: dimly I saw one of the hooped bridges going over to it and a small boat, too, moored by the side. 'Your grandmother lives here?' I said, knowing I sounded stupid. The house, clearly an original Japanese concoction, was made of paper. Even the most eccentric English grandmother, I thought, would be unlikely to live here.

Amy shook her head. Then she pulled off her shoes and beckoned to me to do the same. 'No, no,' she said, as we went barefoot through grass that had a good deal of wetness in it, dew perhaps, or water from the hoses of Lovegrove gardeners, keeping the exotic collection of trees and shrubs in perfect condition, 'my grandmother is dead. She built little houses everywhere. I told you, Jenny, I found one I'd never seen before, last holiday. In the big wood. I'll take you. But it's spooky there, I warn you!'

Amy was clearly enjoying herself, and was once more, I thought, like a younger child, conspiratorial, whispering even, so that the illusion of the shuffles and murmurs of the old Imperial Court came once more irresistibly to mind.

'She was very extraordinary,' Amy went on. A curious mixture of defiance and defence was in her voice. I was to hear it often when she talked of her family. I felt, then, that I had been tactless and that Amy was still grieving for her grandmother, hadn't wanted to mention this extra-terrestrial being at school. 'I'm sorry,' I said, knowing I sounded clumsy. 'When did she . . . die?'

Amy gave a short sigh. At the same time a flight of duck went up the stream where the little boathouse stood. Their wings gave off a theatrical clap and I felt suddenly the last thing I had expected: a pang of homesickness for Aunt Babs, and the old chintz curtains pulled against the mews at the back, and the sound of the stalls, some of them still horse-drawn, leaving a litter of old cabbage leaves and heading home. 'She died ages ago,' Amy said. 'I mean, I never knew her, she died about fifteen years before I was born. But she made all this, you see –' Amy gestured to the back of Lovegrove, the sprawling, bulky, seemingly unending house which had yet a Hall of such complexity that I thought I would never be able to find my way along the landings that led off the stairs feeding from it. Amy turned to embrace the garden too. 'She made the garden. Her father designed the house – with a great architect, Philip Webb. And there were these little houses everywhere.' Now Amy was half-way down to the river bank. I followed her, stepping as silently as I could in the grass that was longer as it approached water, and thick with daisies and clover. 'She loved it here' – Amy turned to me as we reached the boat. The moon had risen and I saw its reflection in the water, lying like a ball of pale wool by the long needle of the oar.

Before Amy could go on, I knew then even more strongly that I didn't want to cross the flimsy bridge to the house that was a home to the boat and a home, too, no doubt, to anyone fanciful enough to wish to spend the night there, over rushing water and protected by walls of paper and cane. I remembered I'd promised Aunt Babs I'd ring to say I'd arrived safely, a fact which had been rubbed out of my mind by the strangeness of the arrival at Lovegrove. (And anyway, where would the telephone be in such a place? I thought of twisting subterranean passages and an ancient implement on the wall, and in this I was proved right.)

Amy started to untie the boat. 'I'll show you the little house when it's light,' she said. 'I knew we'd miss it. I'll take you down the stream now and out on to the Love and as far as the weir where it meets the Avon,' she said. 'Wouldn't you like that, Jenny?' She may have seen me hesitate; for, as if to give validation to her offer, she said, 'My grandmother used to go out at night in the boat – in this boat – and she used to take the children with her.'

'That sounds lovely,' I said, with as much assurance as I could find in me.

'They all loved her so much,' Amy said. She had grown thoughtful. The rope, pretty ancient by the look of it, which she had just untied from the mooring pole, dangled in her hand. As for me, I could have sworn I heard something louder than a rustle – it was like a breath, or two breaths caught and coming out together; and something primitive in me felt a presence, behind my back, in the clump of bamboo, a panther, possibly, in this paradise. As it turned out, I even had the direction wrong.

'My grandmother loved children,' Amy said. She had clearly heard nothing. But her zeal for what she was saying made her voice rise above a whisper. Again, it sounded rather piping and childlike, slightly plaintive. 'She built all the little houses for the children, you see, Jenny. And they loved her so much too.'

I must confess I was hardly able to handle this. It was so unlike the Amy at school, the cool, non-committal Amy who caused the same kind of passions to be kindled in the breasts of adolescent girls: and all for a dead grandmother! It occurred to me that Lady Lovescombe must have something to do with this: her own coolness to Amy had been remarkable. But I said nothing, of course. I hoped only that something would come to stop the trip down the river. It was unlike me, or so I thought until then, to mind the chance of freedom, escape, even a bit of adventure, after the long, bland weekends with Aunt Babs, collecting things together for her stall, exchanging the same jokes with the same women, straggly-haired, beak-nosed, blue with cold in the early mornings in the Portobello Road. There, I would have prayed for this: a stream which went down through Chinese gardens to meet the wider, faster-flowing Love; Amy at the oars, all the finery of the poplars and the weeping willows picked out silver in the moon. Instead I felt only a kind of sick boredom, which much later I was able to identify as an unease – or disease – caused perhaps by too much exposure to the Lovescombe family.

In the event, something did happen to stop the boating trip, but it gave my heart such a lurch at the time that I'd rather have gone on the river. It was what appeared at first to be a ball of black twigs, unconnected though with a tree or with any visible support on the ground; it moved across the small hump bridge from the boathouse, and at the speed of a cannonball too, so that I let out a muffled scream – muffled by Amy's hands over my mouth, for she had seen it too. We both dropped down into the long grass. Prickles dug into the sides of my feet. A cloud of pollen came up out of the clover and I felt the beginning of a sneeze.

The ball of twigs grew a pale column as it came closer.

Amy's fists were clenched in the long grass, and I thought that she rather than I was going to let out a sound – that she would take over my sneeze and sneeze as she had in Miss Carston's art-room – a great, bellowing, trumpeting sound that would frighten away the horror of the part-human, part-ghost, a face as white as a Noh mask, black hair knotted and standing out like the end of a witch's broom. But the vision, coming nearer and then passing us in our burrow, brought nothing from Amy but a long sigh. The naked form, almost pearlized, waxy and with a black triangle at the base of the slender stomach ran into a clump of bamboo and disappeared. I waited for Amy to move. She sat on, very tense, as if she had forgotten how to stand or stretch her limbs.

'What was that?' I managed, in as low a whisper as I could.

Chillingly, a laugh came from the bamboo clump and a sound of scuffling. Amy's fists unclenched at last and she stood up. 'I'm going, Jenny. Round to another door. A side door.' And she set off across the grass. I struggled to reach her. 'But what?' I said. Amy turned to face me, and I knew I had offended her – deeply offended her, even – that I might as well leave Lovegrove on the evening I'd come, that I had no place here and hadn't learnt that to come to a place like this was to keep quiet, keep the head low. ('We don't know anything about them,' Aunt Babs had said. How crass of me to think that newspaper reports of Lord Lovescombe's art collections, or of Lady Lovescombe, one of the ten best-dressed women in the country etc., etc., and her trip to Paris, her new Givenchy balldress for the coming-of-age of their son Ludo . . . where all the glittering people would be: the princesses, politicians, peers . . . How crass of me to think therefore that by reading this trash we *did* know them, when in fact we'd made the mistake all obscure people make when it comes to the famous. We had the same sense of knowing them as if they were ourselves.)

Amy had refused to answer my question and sped away. I couldn't see her now, in the dark. But the two words she had said had the same hiss to them as when uttered in the drawing-room, in front of a stony Lady Lovescombe: 'Jasmine Tremlett!'

The rest of that early part of the evening remains obscure in my mind. It was the sinking feeling, I suppose, that Amy had run off into the fabric of Lovegrove, finding a hole that would admit her, whereas I must go back up the steps to the french windows to the drawing-room – which Amy hadn't wanted to do and which I therefore dreaded as well, for reasons social, paranormal, or for any reason you like in the state of heightened awareness I was in. It meant passing the clump of bamboos, of course (and although I knew it was Jasmine Tremlett rather than some Oriental beast concealed there, I had as little desire to go past as if it had been a panther after all. Worse, I couldn't believe the excessive rustling coming from the clump could belong to one person, even if, following some tradition which I now knew I must never inquire into if I wished to remain at Lovegrove, there was a transformation of a very compli- cated nature in progress, such as a whale-boned and multi- buttoned zippered creation going on. Chuckles coming shortly after this seemed to make a solitary change even more unlikely; and indeed I did see what I (and presumably Amy even more) had dreaded seeing – a stout man, in a black suit very probably, as his body was virtually invisible in the dark, hurrying from the bamboo and on to the steps of the french windows. He turned once, searching for Jasmine Tremlett I suppose, and I saw a heavy-set face with a low brow and thick black eyebrows going over a wide, pudgy nose. The face was aggressive, determined, but also criminal, I thought: furtive. The wild possibility that this was a burglar, or gangster of some kind, who was known to Amy as the consort of the unappetizing Jasmine Tremlett, but of whom her hosts were unaware, causing the necessity for clandestine rendezvous in the boathouse, crossed my mind. Why such secrecy? And, if this were the case, surely Amy's distaste for such behaviour in the grounds of her own home would be justified. Did Jim Tremlett know? Yet the possibility seemed somehow remote. I remembered that these were the kind of people who went to the night-clubs sometimes mentioned with a light laugh of derision by Aunt Babs: the Gargoyle very likely, more than the Ivy or Quaglino's, all of which had fascinated my early imagination. 'Lucian Freud and Philip Toynbee and all that sort,' said Aunt Babs, who, I was able to think much later, would, given her artistic inclinations, have very much liked to join them. 'And Bernard Ehrlich gets drunk there every night, I gather.' (It was never clear where Aunt Babs did her 'gathering', but the Portobello Road wasn't short on this type of gossip, though the stallholders, other than via the handling of stolen goods, some of which might come from Lovegrove or somewhere like it, would be likely to know little of the actual lives of people like the Lovescombes.)

Jasmine Tremlett, having emerged from her bush, but in a 'little black dress', disappointingly, rather than a Creation, joined the thickset man on the steps to the drawing-room. They then appeared to have a short, whispered conference, which resulted in the man vanishing, as Amy had done, down the other side of the steps and into the darkness, over the maze of streams and little bridges. Jasmine Tremlett paused, then opened the long door (which meant pushing against heavy brown brocade curtains) and stepped in. I waited a short while, which felt like an age, and then, hoping in another fit of panic that she hadn't locked the door behind her, I went up the steps and did the same. The door opened easily. A faint breath of roses and syringa from the tall vases, mixed with cigarette smoke, met me as I pushed against the curtain. My heart was thudding in a ridiculous way. But the drawing-room, tidied by unseen hands in preparation for the evening proper, was completely empty. Everyone, I thought miserably, must be having a bath and getting ready for dinner: even Jasmine Tremlett, perhaps, was changing yet again, just to keep her hand in. I went to the door Amy and I had come through what seemed several hundred years ago. And out into the hall. A question of picking your staircase, I thought and, heading for the nearest grass-green flight, I did.

CHAPTER FOUR

'Walter Neet.'

The man outside the first door in the main bedroom passage (as I assumed it to be) seemed all the smaller and more rotund for the height and elegant length of the room half-visible behind him. His heavy jaws, which had the look of used chewing-gum, hung, then writhed in an equally putty-coloured face. Hairs sprouted from his nostrils. Despite all this he had a kind of swagger, a Napoleonic gait as he came towards me in the gloom. 'You look lost. It's a bit of a speciality of mine, guiding those who have been let down into the ninth circle of Hell or thereabouts by one of the Lovescombes, into their allotted place. An extraordinary thing, a sort of forgetfulness, wouldn't you say? As if everyone was born with the layout of Lovegrove in their minds, as if it were latently *there* in all sentient beings, so to speak, and had only to be coaxed into showing itself on the occasion of a first visit. Nobody told you where your room is, I take it?'

I shook my head, taken aback (and, truth to tell, quite upset by Amy's clear dread of at least some of the people she was going to be shut up with for an indefinite time). Walter Neet, whoever he might be, was almost more than I could take on board at present, and the homesickness returned with a pang, so that I had to remind myself that I could ring Aunt Babs at any time and use the money she had given me (five pounds, a princely sum in those days and expected to 'get me through the holidays') for a taxi to the station and a train home. But Walter Neet was probably the only person who could help me, in a house that had such a thick silence, so hushed a pre-prandial air that it would be somehow unthinkable to open a door at random, come in on suspender belt and handmade lingerie, a husband and wife dressing together perhaps, the clasping on of a necklace, the tying of a tie. I shrank from the prospect of any of this.

'Certainly I should know my way around,' said Walter Neet, rolling his jowl like a pair of rubber mats, pulling them in again and then giving, when they had come to rest, a strange smile, as straight as the bristly but small moustache across his lower face. The jaws and chins took and buried this smile, as crags and cliffs would an unwary centipede or creepy-crawly. The door behind him, guided by his body, swung open further, to reveal a splendid room, with four-poster, curtains in watered grey silk, walls in a pale grey that showed off architectural drawings, Italian monasteries in Victorian gouache, views of (presumably) Lovegrove before the Chinese garden had been built, with straight lawns, the cedar before the need for the iron prop, the river behind nothing more sensational than water in a clump of reeds. An easel also stood in the room, surprisingly perhaps, and a simple chair was beside it, with palette and brushes. There was a strong smell of turpentine.

'Extraordinary, what they've done to this place,' said Walter Neet. 'I'll show you my sketches of house and grounds in a minute. It's nothing to do with the Rudds, of course, all this chinoiserie. The Rudds would never have gone in for this sort of thing.'

I dimly remembered the occasion at St Peter's, early on in Candida's 'crush' on Amy, and while I was still ignorant of these things, so important, it appeared, to Candida, when she had turned on me with scorn at my mention of 'Amy and Mr and Mrs Rudd'. 'That's not right,' she hissed (we were in an English lesson, I think, and the mystifying Shakespearian titles, Earl, Marquess, Baron, had come under scrutiny, much to the boredom of everyone in the class except Candida Tarn). 'Rudd is the *family* name,' she'd said, angry enough with my stupidity and uncaringness to risk a reproof. 'Her parents are the *Lovescombes*. Lord Lovescombe's grandfather was made a peer. The present viscount's heir is the Honourable Ludo Rudd.'

'You must be Amy's friend,' Walter Neet said, as if this had only just crossed his mind. I said I was, and said my name was Jenny Carter.

'Jenny Carter,' said Walter Neet, as if this information was utterly perplexing. 'Well, Jenny, you're going to have to tell me whether Amy is as forgetful as some of the other members of the family. Mind you, some might label it egomania. None of that comes from the Rudd side, either. Certainly they were pushing, hard-headed, built themselves up in industry. But they were too busy doing that, y'know, to spend much time on themselves. Unlike the Azebys. Good God, no. You've heard of the Azebys, Jenny, I dare say?'

I had to dare say I hadn't. Walter Neet shook his head, even more baffled by my origins, my apparent life in outer space without hearing so much as a whisper about the Azebys. 'You can't have done very much history then,' he said in a disappointed tone. 'Henry Azeby was in Balfour's administration. Virginia Azeby, his wife, built Lovegrove, she encouraged such artists as Dante Gabriel Rossetti, such great craftsmen as William Morris, to put their stamp on this magnificent house. And of course she worked closely with Philip Webb on the actual architecture of the house.' He paused for breath, avoiding my eye in case he saw the vacant look of the member of another race told suddenly the intricacies of the rules of their new country. 'The Azebys have always been *special*. I'm sure you know what I mean? No one has ever been able to know why they think themselves all *that* special. But they do. Then Virginia Azeby's daughter, Marguerite – well, of course she married a Rudd. She was an only child – title passed down in the female line. Rudd was made a peer in the First War: took Lovescombe to fit in with his wife's estates. So much money!' Neet blew out his cheeks so that two puffballs jumped from them in a vain attempt to parachute away. The porous, beige protuberances went slowly down as he stepped backwards into the room, flinging the door further open and disclosing an assortment of watercolours of Lovegrove executed in a spiky, anodyne style, with flowers on the terraces very much to the fore and the Chinese garden mistily seen, primulas and wild forget-me-nots obscuring the more garish tones of the little bridges. 'Nice, aren't they?' Neet remarked before I had time for a polite comment. 'A commission I'd been looking forward to, I may say.' He let out another succession of brown cannon-balls from his jowls, this time making a popping noise as they subsided. 'But the Lovescombes are forgetful. Well, it comes from the Azebys, of course. Anne Lovescombe simply took over the whole thing when she married Rich-ard Lovescombe: she had no idea of this sort of style, she just picked it up in the last few years that Marguerite Azeby was alive. What a mother-in-law to have to live up to, some people said. Marguerite a Soul and all that –' again Neet averted his eyes from my foreigner's ignorance. (And I couldn't help briefly wondering what Candida Tarn, the true foreigner, would have made of all of this, until I reflected that Candida, very likely, would know just what a 'Soul' might be.) 'No, she just took to it like a fish to water,' Neet said. 'Anne Lovescombe was an Azeby before one knew where one was. Only trouble is' – he picked up a brush from the chair and made play with it, as if feinting with an imaginary adversary – 'the famous forgetfulness goes with it. I mean, Jenny, you look a sensible girl. What would you say these pictures would fetch on an open market? No – well . . .' Neet plunged on, having caught, finally, my bewildered look, 'No – well you wouldn't know I suppose. All I can say is that I was promised an *advance* of £250 – an advance, mind you, representing a half of the price to be paid for the commission. And now I am told that that is *all* I am getting. That I agreed, even, to this monstrous price. Wouldn't you say that was *very* forgetful, Jenny?'

A gong sounded somewhere in the depths of the Hall, the roar coming up the thick carpet of the stairs like a distant crash of cutlery-laden trays. I turned, nervous: the rest of the house was so quiet still that it was as if the gong, by breaking the silence, had broken some ancient taboo that had had everyone asleep for over a hundred years. 'But at least it's rather a change, staying here,' Neet allowed. He stood aside, making visible the white-quilted four-poster, on which an indeterminate garment had been carefully arranged. 'They know one likes to paint at night sometimes. It's not everywhere one has one's smock laid out for one,' Neet said.

After being shown along the passage by Walter Neet to a room where a small card, set into a gold card-holder on the door, proclaimed 'The Honeysuckle Room', and told that the gong that had just gone off was 'only the dressing gong' and there was plenty of time before dinner, I set out to discover what had happened to my clothes. At first sight, these, along with the suitcase, seemed to have disappeared. The mahogany chests of drawers, of which there were three as well as a wardrobe, could have held the outfits of an army of trolls. Empty, paper-lined drawers gave a sense of growing insecurity so that I had to fight back tears. How could I 'go down' to dinner with nothing to wear? What would Aunt Babs say if she discovered I had had to creep home because my brave new friend had, first, lost sight of me altogether and second, instructed the maids to jettison my clothing in return for my tactless behaviour? Then I remembered that one of the features of Lovegrove was its abundance of doors, some apparently leading to other rooms and passageways and others, as in the case of the 'book-lined' door by the writing-table in the drawing-room (where the spines of the books were inscribed with such titles as *Handel On The Art of Turning*), revealing that they were merely cupboards. This turned out to be the case in the Honeysuckle Room to which I had been consigned. A door behind a curtain (which I had assumed must conceal a window) opened straight into a deep cupboard, where my few cotton dresses were hanging, and shelves where the rest of my things were neatly stacked. To the left of this curtain another door revealed a bathroom, where what looked like nine feet of water lay in the bath and a towel which was also troll-sized was draped over a chair by the side of the bath, itself at least the length of a giant's burial site. On my toothbrush, which reclined on the marble edge of a heavy wash-hand-stand-basin, was a snake of toothpaste: not mine, I realized with a rush of shame, for this was from a different tube from Aunt Babs' Macleans, which

I now clearly remembered leaving behind in the bathroom at home. The presence of the towel and toothpaste allayed my doubts that someone else had just been in the bath and failed to let out the water. I had been prepared for, there was no doubt about it; and whether it was late or not I felt honour-bound to undress and climb in. A bottle of Floris Rose Geranium bath essence stood conveniently to hand and I poured in a careful trickle. It was impossible to lie back in the bath without total submersion, and I sat as upright and rigid as it occurred to me, sensing my own posture, Candida would have done, given similar circumstances. Just as self-consciously I washed myself with a flossy white flannel provided by the house – my own having horribly failed, doubtless, to come up to required standards – and got out to wrap myself in the gargantuan winding-sheet.

How one can tell one is being watched is hard to say. The air at Lovegrove was beginning to be suffocating in its silence, it was true, and I was alert to the slightest movement. But there is something else: an eye in the back of the head or whatever it may be; and if this had been proved wrong in its direction with the clandestine lovers in the garden, here it told me with an insistence on its accuracy that the keyhole of the door that led from the bathroom to the hushed, wood-panelled corridor contained another eye; and a painter's eye at that, though I had little interest in the aesthetic value of the experience at the time.

I rose from the chair and went into the Honeysuckle Room next door. Once again Aunt Babs, whose hopelessly puritanical and out-of-date ideas I had brushed aside, had been right: 'Lovegrove,' she'd said, when I first mentioned the name of the place. 'Notorious for the "pretty women" who went there. Everyone slept in someone else's room, and a gong went off at 7 a.m. to get people back to their

47

spouses' quarters. Edward VII stayed there, of course. There were great battles between the ethereal Lady Azeby and her brash sister-in-law, Charity Rudd, about the goings-on there. Marguerite Azeby would have preferred her spiritualist seances to all the chamber-swapping any day, but the house certainly had that reputation.' Seeing Aunt Babs was still half reproving me for accepting the invitation, I used my only weapon on her, which was to ask how she knew so much about these people about whom she knew nothing. 'It was different in the old days,' was all Aunt Babs would say. 'My mother used to hear things.' And with this intimation of an infinitely smaller society, with its clearly defined hierarchies and closed and open doors – some of them, as at Lovegrove, doors that led nowhere or gave the impression of opening into society, while in fact leading the outsider to no more than a dead end – Aunt Babs closed the subject.

None of this, however, could have much bearing on my present predicament except to make me fear, with an intensity I hadn't yet known, the sounding of a gong which would release Walter Neet, as at some secret signal known only to the initiates, into the Honeysuckle Room and thus, as a practitioner of a well-known pre-dinner sport of the naughty nineties, on to myself. I went as fast as I could to the cupboard where my clothes were kept; and in my nervous apprehension I dressed myself from top to toe inside it. I then opened the door into the main bedroom passage, which stretched out before me as empty and innocent as before. Scenes of almost Hogarthian licentiousness suggested themselves to me as I made for the distant staircase I had come up. But more important than thinking of these was the necessity of finding the dining-room. Unless there were 'drinks before dinner' in the drawing-room first? I tried to remember what it had been like when my parents took me to stay with old Colonel Forbes, a relative of my mother's in the north of Scotland. Had we all assembled before going in to eat? Had we had 'drinks before dinner' first? I had no idea. At Lovegrove, anyway, there seemed to be no choice. I had no idea there, either; but also no idea of where the dining-room might be. I turned at the end of the green flight of stairs into the green hall and set off in the known direction of the drawing-room.

CHAPTER FIVE

Here at least were signs of recent occupation. Cushions had been sat back against. A copy of *Country Life* lay open on one of the magnificent white sofas. Square glass ashtrays that looked as if they could house a shoal of fish if required had here and there received cigarette ends. Glasses with rinds of fruit, some gnawed, bitten and spat out, stood about on tables which held also white china vases of sweet peas; receptacles in the shape of swans or hands contained sweet williams, lupins, love-in-the-mist. There was an air of gentle debauch, to be corrected any minute no doubt by tidying, rustling maids. For the moment, though, the tall mirror (later to be explained by Walter Neet as a 'ludicrously overdone piece of Chinese Chippendale') reflected the mild debris of the drinks-tray on the lacquer table at the far end of the room. Stoppers were out of the wide decanters of whisky, sherry and brandy; a jar of crystallized cherries stood open with a dribble of red juice going down its side on to a black papier-mâché tray; a dish of nuts had spilled, too, as far as the patterned and garlanded carpet on the floor, so that a suggestion of an abandoned zoo, or an aviary at least, came over in the none-too-fresh air. This in turn held a clash of scents, of which the strongest had a heavy, musk-like tone that mingled with the gin and remains of smoke; Jasmine Tremlett's, I thought, though I had no memory of smelling it on her in the garden when she had flitted past me to the drawing-room steps. However, as there was no sign of Jasmine Tremlett, or indeed of anyone else, there was no way of confirming this.

I think it was at that moment that I gave up hope of being able ever to understand or master Lovegrove. I knew I would never find Amy or any of the others. For all I knew I was hopelessly late for dinner and would be expelled by Lady Lovescombe, who had already rung my Aunt Babs and asked her to send for so uncivilized a guest and remove her altogether. I hadn't the courage to go out in that Great Hall again and try my luck at all the doors, some of them imposing and 'double', as if they led to reception rooms of ambassadorial proportions, others very likely revealing more hidden staircases which might lead me to a part of the house entirely forbidden to people like myself. I stood on, as if thrown into an enchanted sleep – as I had thought earlier of the rest of the household – but in my case the spell had fallen while I was in the wrong place, and worse, with everyone else now woken, for how could the sleeping make such a mess of things as, in so short a time in the drawing-room, they had? I stood gazing into the depths of the extra-ordinarily ornate mirror, where the fanfares of flowers from the tall vases fused in reflection with the gilded birds and salamanders of the frame, giving giant poppies, peonies and arum lilies a background of unexpected richness, like an Oriental hanging.

The mirror just showed the long sofa at the far end of the room by the drinks-tray. What I had taken to be an assortment of crumpled cushions on an expanse of white linen moved slightly. There was a loud hiccup. A hand that was almost impossibly long and thin stretched out for a decanter; and suddenly the unstoppered condition of all three seemed more plausible, my first reaction to this having been that it would be most unlike Lady Lovescombe to lead her guests in to dinner and leave all that drink carelessly open behind her. The decanter swayed dangerously now, in the long hand. I knew I had to turn, away from this surreal picture of reclining drinker, lilies and poppies in a golden surround, and confront the real thing. But something in me was still frozen, asleep, and I stared on.

'Capitalist bitch!' said a voice from a head that was still invisible, concealed by a blue linen cushion piped in white. The head then slowly appeared, preceded by a straggle of hair and the upper part of a face that was filthy by any standards: what my Aunt Babs would have called 'I'm afraid in need of a good wash', which was her way of both drawing attention to a tramp and expressing compassion for him and his general lack of amenities. For here was a tramp indeed. The lower part of the face, emerging from behind the cushion in order to swig at the neck of the decanter, was even more dirty-looking by virtue of a half-grown moustache, which wandered, apparently at will, down the sides of the mouth and then suddenly up again, as if a slapdash attempt had been made to twirl or wax the points. Unlike Walter Neet's moustache in this respect, it was also different in colour, being a dramatic black, as if the effect desired was that of a dressing-up-box version of a Spanish gypsy. The mouth under all this was both long and thick, with teeth that seemed both black and yellow, or, possibly, in the case of the black, simply missing. This would in turn account for the slurred, indistinct way of talking, which was more wild and unexpected than the speech of most drunks (that I'd heard, at least, brawling outside the Portobello Road pub after closing time): the words came out as if blown by a strong and, as I was soon to discover, malodorous wind – the windy gaps, seemingly, producing most of the breath.

'*She* says we come between this date and that date. *She* says we bring the children. *She* says where they have breakfast, when they have tea, no running in the hall. Stupid bitch could be running a girls' school. And she thinks she's Marguerite Azeby. Snobs, Fascists, the lot of them, always were, but I'll tell you one thing, Marguerite Azeby *loved* children.'

As he finished, legs that were as impossibly long and thin as the hands uncrossed like a pair of scissors and brought the strange spectacle of a dinner jacket apparently put on back to front, and grey flannel trousers, as disastrously stained as the coat, to a standing/leaning position by the drinks-table. The stopper from the whisky decanter crashed to the ground as, with enormous care, and walking as if negotiating a field of writhing snakes, this figure bore down on me. Before long I could smell the breath, which gave off a reek impossible to describe, and see the face, which was hideously scarred, as if a duel had resulted in some careless drawing with a blade on the part of the successful opponent. 'I hate all that stuff, don't you? All the class privilege dressed up as sentiment – all that sort of thing –' Surprisingly, the figure came to a halt about a foot away from me. (I had thought, I suppose, that this was the last of me, in this strange initiation into the ways of Lovegrove, that I would be attacked, felled by a drunk madman in a room that no one would bother to revisit that evening, there being so many others to choose from.) On the contrary, obeying perhaps some half-blurred idea of a 'correct' distance at a cocktail party, the inhabitant of what I now saw to be a dog-collar and black shirt-front – rather than a dinner jacket backwards as I had thought – came to rest about a foot away from me. The smell added considerably to the lingering aroma of menagerie or travelling circus in a room designed to receive only the pale smells of garden flowers or just-bathed women.

'What are *you* doing here?' said this unlikely vicar, looking round with the air of someone who is in fact at a cocktail party, taking in the presence of other guests, swaying with the crowd. 'You're trying to run away too, aren't you?' The face came briefly very near, letting out from the gashed skin a cheesy stench this time. 'You know how Mary and I ran away – 'course you do.' A laugh that may have been intended as self-deprecating or may simply have got caught up in the gaps in the mouth came out in belches. 'Not married in church, I can tell you. That's why I thought I'd put on this outfit tonight, just to annoy her Ladyship. Oh no, you couldn't get further from the Lovescombe marriage, with Mary and me. You couldn't get two sisters more different either. Pompous ass, Anne Lovescombe. Not that Mary's got a brain in her head, it must be said. Let the children do without seeing a lot of snobs is what I say. But Mary must come here. Spain. Married –' He suddenly went on at speed, as if sensing an imminent interruption, possibly punishment from approaching staff. 'We stopped on the way to the Spanish war . . . married in Nice . . . well, we had to have a bit of a honeymoon before facing up to old Franco, don't you see . . .'

A voice that was clear and clipped, reminding me with sudden unpleasantness of the voices of many of the mistresses at school, broke in on the soliloquy. I saw then the analogy between those two institutions, the college for young ladies and the 'great country house' as it had been before the war, and in the case of Lovegrove, remained. 'Unsuitable', but for one reason or another necessary members of the household, such as Walter Neet or the strange apparition who claimed to be Lady Lovescombe's brother-in-law, were closely monitored, as would be the art-master, dancing-master or, to look for an analogy with this no doubt unwelcome addition to the family, the defrocked chaplain who on grounds of a buried scandal within the school cannot be released into the outside world. The cool voice came again, showing in its crystal cadences the contempt and patronage felt by one dependant for another – in particular by the hard-working employee for the idle parasite. Miss Bolt – for so it was, as I guessed from the fleeting glimpse earlier in the hall – had found the stopper of the decanter on the floor and was replacing it with a glassy click as she spoke. 'Mr Crane, Lady Lovescombe is expecting you at dinner.'

Miss Bolt was small and compact. Her eyes travelled over the shambles of the tardy guest and then turned on me. 'You'd better follow me, Jenny,' she said. 'Amy wanted to come and find you but Lady Lovescombe doesn't like her table disturbed all the time.' Something in Miss Bolt's tone now reminded me of Candida Tarn at her most ingratiating with the mistresses at St Peter's, when her tone came cloyingly close to their own. I must have looked hesitant, for Miss Bolt now snapped: 'No one could think where you got to, this evening. Dinner is being served.'

'Blotted our copybooks again,' Crane said happily. 'And just when you thought you could run off with the family jewels, eh? Jenny, is it? Good for you, Jenny!' In his attempt to pat me on the back, Crane tottered and lurched into a side table, which in return disgorged a vase in the form of three white kittens with bows around their necks and an arrangement of marigolds and spray roses. Unhurt by the thick carpet, the kittens rolled to Miss Bolt's feet. The drawing-room door opened and a flotilla of maids came in before anything could be said of the incident, Miss Bolt standing in the floral spill like Demeter deciding not to go down into the underworld. 'Time for a spot of dinner,' Crane said, trying now to take my arm and 'lead me in', but missing by several feet and flailing instead, an action which appeared by the wind it created to propel him to the door. I followed as the maids, trained, I supposed, to pay no attention to such small matters as drunken guests or husbands and wives making wild guesses as to their real spouse in the unkind hour of early-morning tea, kept their eyes away from both of us.

'Food's disgusting but one's got to eat something,' Crane said, as I went after his stick-insect dance across the grassy expanse of the Philip Webb hall to the dining-room.

CHAPTER SIX

There are some occasions so embarrassing that, even at a distance of more than thirty years, the acute agony can return, brought by a phrase, a whiff of scent, a certain ambience even, in a restaurant: dark walls, a grouping of wine bottles on a sideboard, a portrait of a woman in white drapery, herself draped against a Grecian column; and all the symptoms are there again, the heat that runs in shafts down the side of the neck, the panic need to flee and the knees that have turned to jelly.

Why that evening at Lovegrove should count as the most painful and frequent of revenants I don't know. Perhaps because it was the first of such occasions for me, and stayed like some ghastly reminder of a lost virginity, popping up at the sound of a certain kind of voice, awakened by the shape of the back of a head or a sudden sideways look at a stranger. Whatever it was, the nucleus of people gathered in the dark-walled room – green I think, dark green as the velvet smoking jacket of the man with his back to the door, in a tall chair that looked as if it had been carved from the antlers of a giant deer – were to take up much of my life and thoughts from then, and still do indeed; and as with a first love, gave me a bewildering sense of my own inadequacy, clumsiness and virtual non-existence. For one thing, Lord Lovescombe, as the velvet-jacketed man so clearly was, was also the man who had panted for breath in the bamboo by the river, left a woman alone in the moonlight to fend for herself while disappearing into another part of the house; and, worst of all, had seen me out there too, as his expression on turning in the horns of the great chair and seeing me again made plain. The twisted, rather rubbery lips thickened considerably in a downward pout. A ridge of flesh across the brow – which gave him the slightly unreal expression of a clown who has hastily pulled on a mask with attached hair – contorted itself into a contour-map frown. The chair beside him was empty and a pudgy hand waved to it. I knew somehow that my companion, who had tottered already to the far end of the table, could hardly be the intended occupier of this seat, and my heart sank further. Would I be asked to leave at the end of dinner, keeping quiet at least until then about what I had seen? Or would I be expected to be the sophisticated woman of the world, one of the participants in an infamous Lovegrove house party? Would it be my turn next to stand naked in the cold damp of a Chinese garden on the edge of an English stream and suffer the breathings of Lord Lovescombe? Was this, perhaps, why Amy had been so upset earlier, abandoning me to my fate and unable to warn me in advance of a Bluebeard father, whose mistresses and former schoolfriends of his daughter lay in a mutilated heap in a room somewhere that had quite definitely not been designed for that purpose by Philip Webb? There *was* Amy, at least, in the chair on the other side of the empty one, and I went over and sat down as unobtrusively as possible, feeling nevertheless all eyes on me and on the fierce colour, the same deep red as the claret in decanters on the table, which stained my face and neck.

'Victor, you're very late,' said Lady Lovescombe from the

far end of the table. Between her and her husband stood two gold candelabra the size of small trees. Deer reclined at their feet, satyrs circled the heavy bases and leaves of an exquisite delicacy in both gold and silver fluted out on all sides, thus further obscuring Lord and Lady Lovescombe from each other (a good thing, I thought at the time, in my naïvety, fearing that Lady Lovescombe might too have seen her husband so short of breath on coming in from the garden).

'My dear Anne,' said Victor Crane, as I now knew him to be called. 'One was caught by a damnably long Vespers, one had to get to the end of one's sermon, I'm sure you'll agree.'

'Victor,' said an anguished voice across the table from Crane, who in his filthy dog-collar and stained front had brought a quick laugh from the man I recognized as being Jim Tremlett, and a muttered expression of incredulity from Amalia Drifton, who was directly opposite me. 'Victor, please!'

All this was so far from anything I had imagined as being part of 'civilized life' that it was hard to believe: even harder to think of trying to convince anyone at school – Miss Carston, say, or Candida Tarn – that these eminent people, praised for their donations of paintings and sculpture to the nation and for their munificent contributions to foundations set up for those less fortunate than themselves, could sit down to dinner with a blasphemous drunk, brother-in-law of the host or no. Aunt Babs knew of course of the lingering 'bad' reputation of the past and had wondered doubtless whether a young person left in her charge in the absence of their parents should risk going to such a place. The effect of the war, she must finally have decided, would have brought the same stringent conditions to the Lovescombes as it had to the rest of the population. (It took me a long time to understand that although most people believed, as Aunt Babs did, that a certain way of life in England had gone forever with the war, it did in fact linger on in pockets and was about to reassert itself with astonishing vigour.) There was little time for reflection, however, for a plate of soup had been set before me, just as the empty plates of the other diners were being taken away, and the necessity (another nightmare of that dinner which often comes to me if I find myself in a similar situation) of drinking hot soup quietly and at speed, presented itself. I remember the blur of the white plate and of a white soup lying in it (Jerusalem artichoke, I was to discover later in my visit, and grown in the walled town that was the vegetable garden at Lovegrove), but unknown to me then and therefore startling, so that at the first spoonful I spluttered, as I miserably felt the other diners were waiting for me to do. A blur, too, surrounded the faces at the table, but Amy, feeling sorry for me at last I suppose, said, as I gulped and burned, 'This is Ludo, Jenny. Or at least it might be if he'd turn round and say hello. Hey, Ludo, you pig!'

The face which now leant across Amy's was, at first glance, quite ridiculously like hers. In the haze I was in, I thought I could have seen Amy and a handsome twin, only slightly more masculine than she and with a mocking look I recognized from times at St Peter's when, conspiring with Carmen and feigning the innocence which all the teachers liked to find in her, Amy set up a practical joke – or even, as I was to remember later as I lay in bed that night at Lovegrove – an impersonation of one of the school governors, Lady Pickering. Ludo's eyes, as grey and what used to be known as 'candid' as his sister's, rested on me for a moment and then swept away, but not before showing amusement at my loud inhalations of soup and my flaming cheeks. 'That was Ludo,' Amy said, with a laugh that held,

I thought, a mixture of affection and irritation. 'And I'll tell you later who some of the others are,' she went on in a lower voice, unaware obviously of my encounters in her absence. 'Well, you came in with Uncle Victor. Mummy will be pleased with you for taking the trouble to bring him in.'

This possible suggestion of Victor Crane being of no more importance than a cat or, worse, 'something the cat brought in', wasn't totally inapposite. Partially blocked from view by the swirl of the gold candelabra, flanked by Jasmine Tremlett and his hostess, and seated just under a life-sized portrait of a woman in white draperies, Crane had the appearance of a malign pet, a griffin perhaps, or one of the nameless members of a necromancer's bestiary. His mouth was right down in the soup plate, showing only the alternate baldness and hirsuteness of his scalp, striped in this way like a badger's. Lapping sounds, outdoing even my inexperienced attempts to drink the soup, came up from his plate – which, Vine having interposed himself between the portrait of the woman in white who so dominated the room and the solitary diner, was in danger of being seized away before the contents had quite gone. Vine's thumb, a majestic piece of anatomy, swollen no doubt from the handing of a thousand entrées and as many again of Mont Blanc and assorted desserts, was curved firmly over the top of the plate. Crane lapped on, however, despite the remonstrations of his wife Mary who was impotently placed opposite him (and thus also opposite the portrait of the paragon of sweet manners, ethereality and joy, the cloud-washed woman in white) and half-hearted efforts on the part of Jasmine Tremlett to make him relinquish his plate.

'Come on, Victor,' Jasmine giggled, throwing a glance down to Lord Lovescombe which, due to the mounted guards in gold patrolling the base of his candlestick, he missed. 'Look, we've got something lovely coming next!'

This, I gathered, referred to a large dish, held aloft by a maid in the temporary inability of Vine to perform his role, and from which portions of feathers and twisted claws extruded, not unlike what an innocent onlooker might expect to see sprout from the extremities of Victor Crane. Vine, maddened by the usurping of what was presumably his proudest moment of the day, tugged at the plate; Crane's head, dislodged by this action, lolled on to the table and lay still.

'First grouse,' announced Lord Lovescombe, too used to his brother-in-law's behaviour, presumably, to pay much attention to it, or too keen a sportsman, alternatively, to give up the celebration of an historic moment.

'How absolutely lovely,' Jasmine Tremlett said. 'Are they from Castle Azeby?'

Lord Lovescombe said they were. He looked pleased by the reference; and something dimly in me understood the 'woman who is trying to please' and the outlines of the probable relationship between her and our host at Lovegrove. Jasmine Tremlett was 'bohemian', as even I could see from the slash of purple lips, hoop earrings and magenta scarf which now accompanied the 'little black dress', giving an air of 'Left Bank' and 'Existentialism' as portrayed recently in the papers when talking of the singer Juliette Greco. There could be something unrewarding about living with Jim Tremlett, I thought vaguely. His check jacket, suggesting a prosperous Yorkshire squire, combined with almost threadbare trousers and a general air of desperation and impecuniousness under the *bonhomie* might have pushed Jasmine in the direction of security – not that so worldly a thought occurred to me then, only the air of insubstantiality in the husband. To be told, as I was later by Amy, that 'Jim Tremlett is editor of *Margin*,' meant nothing, suggesting only greater precariousness, if I remember, and it was only much later still that I was to learn how large a part the periodical and indeed both the Tremletts played in the lives of the British 'intelligentsia'. Besides, a battle was breaking out over the grouse – or what seemed a fray of some kind – as Vine went as fast as his heavy butler's tread would allow him, to wrest the platter from the hands of the parlourmaid, the first grouse of the season being far too momentous an occasion to let slip.

Walter Neet was sitting directly under the platter. He had Lady Lovescombe on his left and her sister, distracted almost to the point of frenzy at Crane's somnolent attitude, on his right. 'I would simply love to try my hand at Castle Azeby next,' Neet was saying, his remark addressing the table in general. He wasn't in his smock, as I'd expected, but in a dinner jacket, clearly the property of a much smaller man, which was literally bursting at the seams. Neet's face and neck, never a calm colour, had turned from a rough putty to a deep brick, and various pustules, not noticeable before, had pushed up under the strain. 'One might do some of the mountains at Castle Azeby as they come down into the garden,' Neet pursued his quest. 'It was always the place your mother loved most of all, wasn't it Richard?'

Lord Lovescombe, who appeared to answer to that name, shook his head ill-temperedly. 'My mother liked Lovegrove,' he said with an air of exasperated finality. Then, 'Where's the champagne?' he demanded in a tone that was quite another one: the tone of a man who is never kept waiting. I felt Amy tense slightly at my side; Ludo, who was clearly able to handle these matters better than his sister, pushed out his chair with the promise that he would go and get it. 'Dad, Vine's been a bit tied up,' he said with a laugh, indicating Crane's place at the table. 'Vine, I'll get it, don't worry.'

By this time Vine, who was in the midst of handing Victor Crane's soup plate to the parlourmaid while simultaneously relieving her of the silver dish, had reached a position midway between Walter Neet and Mary Crane. A leg of grouse came down fast, its accompanying garnish of feathers going up in the air as if the bird had just been shot. I saw Amalia Drifton, across the polished stretch of table, watching the scene with a vaguely malicious gleam in her eye.

'How exciting!' cried poor Mary Crane, as the claws, sharp as old heather roots and, with what seemed at a distance to be Chinese-yellow toenails, fastened on her shoulders. 'Did you have a good bag this year?' Mary Crane went desperately on, while small moans, interspersed with 'I'll clear this up' and apologies which seemed totally unnecessary, proceeded also from her. Neet, who had only received a small stream of gravy from the sloping hand of the now-flustered parlourmaid, mopped himself with an air of importance, as if he had just been awarded an accolade or an invitation at least to paint the mountains of Lord Lovescombe's northern seat. 'How disgusting,' Amalia Drifton said coldly. 'Why don't you just leave the grouse in Cumberland, Richard, and make do with some perfectly ordinary food down here?'

This was very typical of Amalia Drifton, as I was to learn; clumsiness was perpetrated frequently in her presence: small, petty, but ludicrous accidents, which she then condemned as if they had been performed on purpose to cause her irritation.

'Oh, *poor* Mary,' cried Jasmine Tremlett. 'It's too bad!'

Mary Crane dealt bravely with the episode (I noted little sympathy from her sister, who was revolted probably at the comatose condition of one spouse and the grouse-spattered state of the other, even if Vine's battle for mastery of the dish had been the cause of the slip). Ludo came in with the champagne and filled our glasses while the platter was arranged. The bread sauce, miraculously, passed over Walter Neet, leaving him relatively unscathed, though a dab, it occurred to me, might have improved his gravy-darkened face. Neet, clearly one of those who are unaware of food or stains left lingering on their faces, talked on, while the eyes of the other diners remained either fixed or guiltily averted from him.

'Of course, that's a magnificent portrait,' said Walter Neet. He waved at the woman in white, a guardian angel now in her setting behind the sleeping Crane. The grouse had made the rounds and very small brussels sprouts, a rarity at this time of year as Lady Lovescombe pointed out, had followed roast potatoes. I dealt with the hairy thighs of the bird as best I could, aware of Amy's mocking look from time to time, and beyond her Ludo's grey eyes leaping at the thought of another guest's misdemeanour on the way. 'Lady Azeby was certainly the most remarkable woman of her time. There was some conflict, I suppose, between the kind of life she wanted here and the life her brother wanted, wouldn't you say?'

'I've no idea,' said Lord Lovescombe, as if he had been asked an intimate question, perhaps one pertaining to the condition of his haemorrhoids. The port, in a decanter which entirely removed the far end of the table from Lord Lovescombe's view – with the exception of a ruby, oval rendering of Crane's face as it lay on the mahogany board – had been placed by Vine in front of him, on a mat encircled by a low silver fence, as if it might be expected in some way to escape, or merely to fall, perhaps, between the fingers of the imbibers.

'It rather makes one shudder,' Neet went on unperturbed, 'to think of all that philistine life going on here, Marlborough House sort of stuff, at the same time as Lady Azeby's séances and writing her books for the children, and all the spiritual side of Lovegrove, which was going on at the other house, Marguerite's house in the woods.'

'I suppose that was a part of the idealism of that circle,' Jim Tremlett put in. 'They were the only people who tried to challenge the assumptions . . . and then, I mean, there was Home Rule and Wilfrid Scawen Blunt and Henry Azeby supporting him in that . . .'

'Votes for women,' Jasmine Tremlett interrupted, although it was unclear as to whether she was advocating this (unaware possibly of developments in the suffrage movement some decades before) or reminding her husband that Lord Lovescombe's famous mother, influenced in all likelihood by the down-to-earth industrialist Rudd, had shown no evidence of a sense of justice when it came to her own son and daughter. Both Lovegrove and Castle Azeby in the north, as Walter Neet had been keen to inform me, passed to Lord Lovescombe on his mother's death, Amalia Drifton occupying the old and landless (and jobless) position of the inheritor's sister.

'Did Marguerite Azeby disapprove dreadfully of the naughty weekends?' asked Mary Crane, with a roguish note, as if to affirm that the wearing of an old chintz dress, a drunken husband and doubtless obstreperous children tucked away upstairs did not indicate an unworldly view of life. 'I mean, it must have been awfully confusing for the servants.'

As if to show his disapproval of the conversation, Vine stepped forward from a deep shadow, lit only by the picture lights of an oil of a windmill in a dismal landscape, and murmured in Lord Lovescombe's ear. At the same time

Lord Lovescombe lifted the decanter from its circlet of silver reeds and pushed it to his left. 'Amy, this is worth having,' he said. His voice sounded tender, almost sentimental. 'Taylor '27. You can't beat this. It is in fact unbeatable.'

It was hard for me to imagine, accustomed as I was to Amy's cool stance at St Peter's, that she could suffer embarrassment – as I could, say, or Candida Tarn, on those occasions when she came across Amy out in the games field, or at a corner by the lab block, somewhere she had been unprepared for and so was incapable of dealing with, a deep colour flooding face and what could be seen of a wide, short chest under an Aertex shirt. (It was Amy's casual, long-legged walk, a pale face that looked almost too grave until a smile suddenly changed it, that gave an impression of a deep, modest sense of who and what she was at a time when we were all struggling to take on one personality or another.) But tonight, at her father's unctuous words, Amy blushed scarlet. I saw she had been drinking some of the claret Vine had poured for us – so had I and, by the looks of it, so indeed had Ludo – and my own colour was still high. Amy's blush, however, came and went as she asked if we might leave the table. I had the feeling she couldn't bear it in there any more.

'I just thought I'd show Jenny something of the house,' Amy said with what sounded like a desperate casualness. 'Do you mind if we go in the Old Drawing-Room, Daddy?'

Lord Lovescombe looked baffled by all this. The port had by now passed down the table and Walter Neet had poured some into his glass. As if reminded of some sacred duty, Lady Lovescombe rose to her feet with a distant expression. At this signal, everyone – with the exception of Victor Crane – rose, Neet with difficulty and with a brimming glass in hand. 'The ladies' then left the dining-room. Aunt

Babs had warned me of this, and I stood to attention nervously, waiting to go out at the end of the queue.

'To the beautiful and fascinating Marguerite Azeby,' said Walter Neet, lifting his glass in a toast to the woman in white, her expression serene still after a dinner which could hardly have been described as satisfactory. 'Sargent knew what he was about, mind you. For that sort of thing, of course,' Neet added hastily. 'One wouldn't dream of painting anyone in that way nowadays. Too soulful.' He gave a short, rumbling laugh, as if his pun had got lost somehow in the glass of port and he was trying to fish it out again. 'And I suppose one could say that people simply don't look like that now. One of the most perplexing problems confronting a painter. Where does a face come from, how does it disappear again? Look at the Pre-Raphaelites . . .'

Headed by Amalia Drifton, the small procession of women left the dining-room. Something slow and regal in their walk suggested a long evening ahead to be enjoyed without the men – or not enjoyed, perhaps, to judge by Jasmine Tremlett's anguished glance at Lord Lovescombe as she passed. Then came Mary Crane, and I couldn't help but wonder at the extraordinary difference between them all: Amalia, though not much more than ten years older than the two other women, probably, was a straightforward copy of the woman in white, her mother – Lady Azeby: white draped evening gown, dark cloud of hair – but without the beauty, a bad-tempered look having seized her face, while her eyes, unlike the wide, grey eyes of Lady Azeby, were a bright, light brown, 'like a bad dog's eyes' as my Aunt Babs would have said. Then Jasmine – I saw that one of her high heels had broken and she half-hobbled from the room, trying to laugh it off – and then Mary Crane, in a flowered skirt and white lace blouse, head down, in flat-heeled shoes and walking as if this evening was just one part of a long night's trudge, as indeed to her it probably was. Lady Lovescombe brought up the rear. I saw as she passed the portrait a fleeting resemblance, as if Lady Lovescombe by dint of sheer effort had come to an arrangement with her late mother-in-law that she could have a certain gracious incline of the neck, a pensive look which helped the features to take on some of Lady Azeby's beauty, a sweep of the shoulders in evening dress which seemed to hold the key to a nature both mystical and exuberant. Then she had walked by. I started for the door, confident that Amy was walking beside me.

'Well, darling?' said Lord Lovescombe.

'I think I'll stay after all.' It was Amy's voice, from her place at table. I turned and saw she had sat down again: the blush had been succeeded by a mulish look. 'Amy wants what's awkward,' I dimly thought. 'She can't be with the others as they expect her to be.' And I saw that it was Ludo who walked beside me to the door. He was in a mischievous mood still – even more so, probably, after the claret – and it crossed my mind that he and Amy 'got up to' tricks like this all the time, to reduce the embarrassment they felt, perhaps, or simply to alleviate the boredom.

'Of course there *is* one very obvious resemblance in the family,' said Walter Neet, still standing and toasting the portrait of Lady Azeby with a glass that had grown considerably more manageable. A slight hold-up at the door, occasioned by Jasmine's heel breaking off altogether, prevented the men from sitting down again. Tremlett, I saw, made no attempt to come to his wife's rescue, aid being given instead by Mary Crane, who supported the guest with a distinctly reluctant look on her face. Jasmine Tremlett, I began to feel, was a woman not much liked by other women. For this reason, with a perversity that was very likely borrowed from Amy, I felt drawn to her. The evening ahead would be best spent as near to her as possible, I decided, if the long hours described by Aunt Babs as lying on the hostess's bed and repairing make-up, discussing one's womb, were really about to unroll.

'It's Jack Hare,' Walter Neet was saying. 'That's who has inherited your mother's looks, Richard. His father was Virginia Azeby's first cousin, of course. The Castle Azeby Azebys. Still, these things jump across families all the time.' As if aware of the fatuousness of his remark, Neet lowered his eyes. A loud hiccup, as startling as if a small gun had gone off, filled the ensuing silence.

'Jack Hare!' said Lord Lovescombe, in a tone of barely suppressed rage. 'Someone we don't see very much of.'

'His last novel was a disappointment,' said Jim Tremlett, as if there were some vague hope in his mind that Lord Lovescombe, after years of abstinence, had read a novel. 'Too . . . I suppose Joycean is the only word that comes to mind.'

At this, Jasmine Tremlett, who had by now removed both high-heeled shoes and was going through the door on Mary Crane's arm (as if a shoeless state had incapacitated her altogether) leant backwards and let out a shrill laugh. 'Really, Jim!' she said. 'Is that what you honestly think? So why publish the entire thing in *Margin*, in that case?'

'That's different –' Jim Tremlett began. But Lord Lovescombe was having nothing more of this protracted postponement of further port. Sweeping me out behind the other 'ladies' he soon had us all in the hall. My last glimpse was of Victor Crane sinking under the table and hiccuping as he went – thus exonerating Walter Neet, at least, from the charge of making these ungainly sounds while lifting his glass to the beauty of the Soul of Lovegrove, Marguerite, Lady Azeby.

I was shut out now from the oval table, and the decanter

of port, and Amy – once again from Amy, who had no wish to see me perhaps, after my encounter with the flitting figures in the garden. Ludo was in the hall with me instead; he turned, dropping away from the train of women as they climbed the stairs slowly to Lady Lovescombe's bedroom. 'I'll show you around a bit, Jenny,' he said. 'And there's ping-pong in the Old Drawing-Room, so we might as well play.'

CHAPTER
SEVEN

Later, when I tried to get to sleep in the Honeysuckle Room, and the plant's tendrils, a fleshy pink and yellow, as endlessly entwined as the ramifications of Amy's family, had woven themselves into my mind, it came to me that, far from my original fear that I would be 'expelled' from Lovegrove – ostensibly for some social misdemeanour but in reality for a failing of personality of which, as in a nightmare, I was unaware – the real danger was that I would never be able to get back into the real world. Not because I had been so hopelessly entranced already that I had no desire to go, and, like the frequently vanishing and reappearing guests, was caught in a long sleep in which a kiss would prolong rather than end the dream; but because, as it seemed to me then, Lovegrove simply didn't exist. Caught in a warp of its own history, a glass dome of time which had somehow been 'blown' by the Lovescombe money, the still-lingering voices of the long-dead lovers – and a rustic Utopia, 'deep feelings', schools for the labourers' children in the red-brick prisons set up for their fathers on the fringes of the willow-strewn estate – Lovegrove would go at the prick of a pin, vanish into the clouds of its own long-lost assumptions. The trouble was, there was no pin to prick it with. Like convicts, we were relieved of all sharp instruments on entering the premises. And, so, of our wits too: though a mocking voice, a sardonic tone, might for a moment obtrude. That night it was the voice of Carmen which came to me some of the time: laughing at the preposterous dinner I had just witnessed (for I could hardly feel I had participated in it); at the self-importance of the hosts, sure as they were of their place in the world, however much that world seemed superficially to have changed; at the pomposity and idiocy of the hangers-on. Yet, as if steeped in a gigantic pool, floating face down beside the developing and self-confirming photographs these people took of each other, criticism seemed out of place. There *was* no other world: the thin rooms at Aunt Babs' seemed empty and bare, not fit to slot in the chests of drawers at Lovegrove. School – apart from the occasional memory, unforgettable because so powerfully anarchistic, of Carmen's bottom as she wiggled and flaunted it outside the Head's room – vanished in a distant smell of disinfectant and apple crumble, fragments of which lodged in the cracks of long refectory tables and under the wainscoting of airless rooms. The past, so rapidly dispersed in the streets of London, the daily rubble of the market where Aunt Babs had her stall – selling the junk of the past, rendering it more harmless still with its mark-ups on the chipped cups the dead had handled: for who *were* these dead, anyway? – was here all-powerful. It was no past of mine, of course, but I was as instantly immersed in it as a heathen in the baptismal waters of an unknown faith. The people who had lived here still lived; and it was possible to see their descendants and their guests as beside the point, actors in a mild charade which could be as grotesque, as 'un-lifelike' as it pleased, for the protagonists weren't those who really lived. It was a frightening thing, to feel, as I did that night, as if I had seen a gallery of ghosts at dinner, that the polite laughter on the upper floor at bedtime had been from another world; yet this was the inescapable conclusion. Did these people, wilfully unaware of the realities of post-war life, 'fake' themselves into a past where they did not in fact belong? Was it this which gave the 'unconvincing' touch to the way they conducted themselves? But was it so unconvincing anyway? It seemed that in surroundings like Lovegrove, any behaviour could be tolerated, because none of it made the slightest difference. The surroundings, and their dead progenitors, were all.

Certainly the 'Old Drawing-Room' had helped to intensify this feeling. Ludo switched on lights to a long room with windows that led out onto a stone balustrade, a mile or so of parquet flooring – rather dusty I noted, as if the room was designated as nothing more than a games room, a forgotten place where the children, even, hardly bothered to come. There was indeed a ping-pong table, rather foolish-looking I thought, on bandy legs in the expanse of wood, listing slightly, as if a slight lurch against it would bring it crashing to the ground. Unsuitably, two fat Chinese vases, each about four feet high and covered with blue and white lotus flowers, stood just behind the table. A 'Dansette' gramophone – I admit I'd wondered, when Amy asked me to stay, if we'd be able to play the new records which were just beginning to seem irresistible to us – sat on the floor, near a mammoth fender and an army of menacing fire-irons. It didn't seem, altogether, the sort of room in which it would be much fun to listen to those strains of a new age.

'Bloody fools lost the bats,' Ludo was muttering. 'Looks as if we can't play after all. It happens every single holidays. Last time I had a bat hideaway' – he gestured at a monumental bookcase, partly bare and partly filled with tall books in dull, dusty bindings. 'But some idiot found them

74

up there and off they went again. Now what d'you think they *do* with them? Beat each other up, I expect.'

It was the first time I'd heard a member of Ludo's race (as I had to see the Lovescombes, Rudds or whatever they might see themselves as) speak of what were clearly still the 'lower orders', and I was shocked. The assumption that some malevolent intention, based on a hardly credible stupidity, was responsible for the disappearance of the table-tennis bats seemed to suggest an inherent understanding of a class war, fought daily on the premises and concealed behind the gracious smile of the chatelaine, Lady Lovescombe. Then I saw the grimy edge of a serrated rubber surface sticking out from behind the 'Dansette' on the floor. I went over and pulled out the bats, almost ashamed of having found them, as if I, too, had been part of this domestics' conspiracy to keep Master Ludo from his game. Straightening, I found myself looking up at the base of a picture that must have been twice my own height, and which reached from the mantelpiece, a forbidding grey marble edifice that was over twice my height already. The picture, as it wasn't hard to see, was of the woman in white again, Marguerite Azeby. This time a group of small children, high above my head, clustered round her.

'Here they are,' I said, holding out the bats. 'I'm not much good, I'm afraid.'

The bashful disclaimer sounded out of place in the room where crinolines and tall hats, coats and long dresses, bustles and chignons dominated the portraits, so that there was, with the fusty smell of an unaired and disliked room, the sense of being shut in a vast costume museum. How could these people care whether or not I was good at ping-pong? Their preoccupations stood out in the scanty light from an overhead gilded chandelier: money, possessions, sometimes the love of children and animals. A certain kind of fluffy dog seemed to have bred with the same regularity as the Lovescombe – or rather Azeby – ancestors.

'Don't let's bother then,' Ludo said. Clearly he had no interest either in the game. Hiding relief, I pointed up at the tall picture over the fireplace, and then at the others, and turned, hoping to be able to get away from Ludo's still mocking eyes and also from the suspicion that he was about to play a trick of some kind on his little sister's friend. To lock me in the Old Drawing-Room for the night, I thought, would be the first thing that would occur to him.

It turned out, however, that Ludo was imbued with less of that dreadful love of horseplay than his background and upbringing might have suggested. He was slightly melancholy, I think; I know, at least, that it was then, letting my eyes fall on him as I turned in front of the pictures, forgetting my decision to get away as soon as possible and go and look for Amy, that I felt a pang for him – the kind of pang a child will feel when left alone in a room, too young to know if the parent will ever return; and I understood then, perhaps, the sense of loss that must always come with the first stirrings of sentimental feeling. Not that I properly understood this, of course: perhaps, at that time, it was the heavy inheritance which hung all round Ludo and which he tried to shake off so unsuccessfully that I did – dimly – recognize and feel sympathy for. He seemed very alone, then, and anxious to be so.

'Cousins,' he said. He waved also up at the gallery of faces, posed bodies, eyes. 'That's what I think of them as, anyway. A pain in the neck, but they keep on coming to stay.'

'Who exactly are they?' I asked, knowing he meant living relatives, a 'tribe' of which I – or Aunt Babs – had no knowledge.

Ludo seemed to dislike my question. He strode to the

door and flicked off the switch. The faces vanished into darkness and a sort of uneasy calm descended on the room, as if our visit had in the first place been a mistake. An after-image of hands, pillars, trees and hair – hair with more life than many of the women subjects, hair plaited, entwined, long as a painted piece of water – stayed with me as I went out into the bright greenness of the hall. As always, there was no sound from anywhere. I assumed the gentlemen – and Amy – were still at the port.

'Ah, there you are,' came the voice of Lady Lovescombe, who had descended the small back staircase that fed into the hall. A glassy organza stole, giving her the appearance of a fairy godmother in a pantomime, stood up around her shoulders. She stood directly facing her son. Ludo, I saw, lowered his eyes. 'Darling, I do want you to play tonight – and Amalia wants you to play. So you will, won't you?'

Ludo nodded. Lady Lovescombe cast a brief glance over me. 'You don't play canasta, do you . . . er . . .'

For some reason I couldn't speak, either to say that Lady Lovescombe was right in imagining that I couldn't play canasta, or to supply my name. I fixed my eyes on the main staircase, a few acres away across the artificial green. At the top lay 'my' bedroom. I decided to get there somehow and wait for Amy to come in search of me.

'I think I'll go up,' I managed to get out.

'Yes.' Lady Lovescombe accepted this without protest. 'Well – goodnight . . .' Her face lifted suddenly. 'Candida. Yes. I do hope you sleep well.'

I woke – and I slept and I woke – on that first night at Lovegrove; and as I slept I dreamt of the past, of what seemed an immeasurable time ago: before Amy said to me, as we stood on the scuffed asphalt outside the school gym,

'Candida's ill, Jenny. Come to Lovegrove if you'd like to.' And then, after issuing this order that had enough tentativeness in it to sound pleading, lonely even, in reply to my stammered question: 'Oh yes, there's plenty of room!'

Perhaps it was because Lady Lovescombe, in her failure to take me in, had made me and Candida – and probably all of the girls at St Peter's – into a kind of amalgam, a monstrous hybrid with blushing faces and 'no conversation at dinner', that I dreamt of Candida above all others that night. I wondered even at times whether she, too, was dreaming of me in the enviable position of dreaming of her at Lovegrove; and, half metamorphosed into her squat body and fresh, hopeful face, I travelled the lines of the No. 27 bus that took me to her house and she to mine: lines her mother and Aunt Babs allowed us to move along on condition we were back at a 'reasonable hour'.

Or we would spend the whole night at each other's houses. The first time, I remember, was an occasion of another letdown for Candida: she had expected to go to Amy's for the night and Lady Lovescombe, at the last minute, had vetoed it.

'There's a ball on, that's why,' Candida said. We were on the top of the No. 27, which was crowded as always with coughing old men and boys from St Peter's, the latter being a species alien and distant, muffler-wrapped, supercilious. Candida had said her own brother had refused to go to St Peter's because of the way the boys there 'turned out', information I took quite seriously at the time. 'It's a very big, very posh ball,' Candida went on. Her eyes had a deadened look, as if she had spent the last night awake, brooding on it. 'Even Amy won't be allowed down.'

'Allowed down?' I had a vision of Amy barricaded on the nursery floor of the by-now legendary house in Primrose

Hill, crying out for a visitor in her lonely eyrie. As it happened, I wasn't so far wrong.

'She can't come down until she's out,' Candida said. 'It's so archaic, it's unbelievable.' Her eyes went brighter, nevertheless, as she dwelt on the subject of Amy's sometimes barbaric fairytale life. 'You know the time I went to tea, Jenny. There was a most terrible drunk there. I wonder if that's really why Lady Lovescombe doesn't let her downstairs on these occasions. And wouldn't let me come, too,' Candida added primly. 'I didn't tell my mother about the kind of people who go there.' She looked at me with a sudden anxiety, as if unhappy at finding a chink in the armour in which she had encased her beloved Amy. 'Of course a lot of very important people go there, too. My father read only yesterday that they entertain cabinet ministers. Lady Lovescombe is some kind of relation of the Churchills.'

Before I had time to flinch from Candida's terrible awe, a hand came down on both our shoulders. I knew, without turning, that it was Carmen Bye; and my heart sank accordingly.

'What's all this about Amy being down and out?' said the teasing, rather deep voice, so useful to Carmen in her many impersonations. 'I should have thought she was doing all right.'

'It's nothing,' said Candida, flushing up as she did when Amy was mentioned by anyone other than herself. 'You've got it all wrong, Carmen.'

Carmen's chuckle turned into a grunt of pleasure as the old man across the aisle from us got up to leave the bus and she slid into his seat. Through the clouds of cigarette smoke she looked at us hopefully. 'Going to your house, Jenny?' (I was considered a much better bet than Candida, Mrs Tarn being notorious for late homework schedules and early revision rises, punctuated by worrying, mid-European food. Nevertheless I looked forward to a night spent away from home, punctuated though it would be, as I could now see, by Candida's longing for the ball at Amy's.) 'If so, I might drop in for a bite.'

It was hard to know where Carmen picked up her expressions. Sometimes foreign-sounding – when she was in gypsy mood – sometimes brisk, almost military, it was thought that despite her protestations of being an orphan, she was in fact the daughter of a French mother and a soldier father. Mail found in her satchel by Candida had shown an address in Aldershot.

'I'm going to Candida's,' I said. 'Sorry, Carmen.'

'You seem to be getting everything wrong today,' Candida said, with the slight smile for which she was by now well-known at school. 'Don't you change here, anyway?' We had arrived at Notting Hill, one stop before Candida's. The boys from St Peter's clattered down the narrow stairs, their navy coats ballooning out and rendering them pompous and suddenly middle-aged, like Belgian bankers falling from the sky in one of the Surrealist pictures my Aunt Babs liked to find (still 'undiscovered' then) at the backs of the attics which provided her stall with its weekly crop.

No one actually knew where Carmen lived. She disappeared sometimes into Notting Hill tube, on other occasions she left St Peter's in the opposite direction from any of us, a direction which contained little or no public transport. There were rumours of a long, white American car, a rarity in those days, waiting round the corner from the sports field.

'Not as wrong as Miss Harland is going to get things tomorrow,' Carmen said with a giggle. 'Amy's lending a hand. Just to show the old pig that she can't be right *all* the time!'

'What d'you mean?' The bus had started up again. The Gaumont Cinema, a temptation which we were forced to resist for fear of reprisals from Mrs Tarn, flashed a grimy poster at the top windows of the No. 27. Today it advertised *The Blue Lagoon*, a forbidden tale of young people in love on an island. Candida stared out at this perplexedly, her lower lip caught between her teeth, as it was when she tried to come top of the class in trigonometry. Carmen stuck out her tongue at the nymph-with-babe and leant back on the seat to enjoy herself. A cloud of dust came off the rubbed, minutely patterned upholstery.

'What I mean is, that tomorrow is Founders' Day. See?'

'Of course I know it's Founders' Day,' Candida said in a stuffy voice. Despite the pretence of long ancestry, St Peter's for Girls had only come into being at the end of the last century. The teachers, delighted at first with Candida leaping to her feet and defending 'The Idea of Tradition' in one of the mock-debates organized in our English class, had become gradually embarrassed by the zeal and loyalty with which she defended these largely bogus traditions. 'For heaven's sake, Carmen, what are you planning to do?'

The arrival of the No. 27 at Candida's stop meant we all had to run down and jump off the platform, Carmen giving the impression at first that she was too comfortable and relaxed to disembark and was settled in her seat for a mystery destination, or possibly simply a round-trip. Then, just as the bus was about to draw away, she ran down and jumped out too. So it was that Carmen inevitably got her way. I imagined Mrs Tarn's face, looking out from her house, munching, as she always was, on bread or cheese, frowning at the arrival of another, unwanted guest. 'You see,' Carmen went on, falling into step with us as naturally as if this evening with Candida had been planned days in advance, 'Lady Pickering is coming to school tomorrow.

And we're all having to give up Break – and Art – to be in the Hall to welcome her. Whaddya know?'

Carmen's sudden Americanisms were intended as a reminder of her glamorous 'GI uncle', who sent her records and even, on occasion, 'candy'. If he was hard to believe in, so were Carmen's renditions of *Oklahoma* or *Annie Get Your Gun*, both of which she claimed had been 'treats' laid on by the Yankee, as she called him, with a pouting expression taken from Doris Day. There was no doubt, however, that Carmen was an excellent mimic and impersonator; and when she went on, casually, 'We've decided to give Miss Harland a bit of a surprise, you see. A sort of double vision. I'm going to be announced as Lady Pickering. And be taken into Miss Harland's study. Amy's going to announce me. You know what a snob Miss Harland is.'

We had reached the turning to the tree-lined street where Candida's parents had settled after their flight from Germany. I thought I could see Mrs Tarn outside the clipped box hedge of the garden, liver sausage and pumpernickel in hand. Something in me wanted to go straight home to Aunt Babs, only one stop up to Notting Hill after all, and then down the vale to Portobello Road and the familiar smells of clearing-away time in the vegetable market. Between them, I thought, Candida and her mother would show their outrage at Carmen. That Candida was already beginning to do so was clear from the greenish colour that had spread over her usually fair, Germanic complexion. Her pale eyes bulged: she looked like one of those fish in the aquarium at the zoo (on illicit visits in the past: Aunt Babs would have nothing to do with the imprisoning of animals) which swim round in what is apparently a perpetual rage, eyes straining and prey always escaping without harm.

'But you can't do that,' Candida spluttered. 'I mean, you'll be *expelled*!'

Carmen started to stride up in the direction of Candida's house. It came back to me that Candida, in her desperate early days at St Peter's, had hung around the gates before they opened in the morning, soliciting for friends. Carmen had been accosted, and with her easy way of accepting any proposition providing it contained something to her advantage, had agreed to go that day to tea. I remembered seeing them set off after school for the No. 27. All this was in the days before Amy hit Candida like some kind of revelation, standing as she did for everything Candida was anxious herself to become. 'And you'll get Amy into terrible trouble,' she went on. I saw the pale eyes mist over with tears, like rain falling behind a window. Candida was foreseeing Amy's expulsion from St Peter's, and a blank desert, unscored by Amy's escutcheon, sunless without her shy, delightful yet quizzical smile, lifeless without the awkward, charming movements of the girl with the long legs and arms of a boy, swam up before her.

But Candida was nothing if not practical. She saw the arrival at her home imminent, and her hand plunged into her satchel for a handkerchief. She had one there, of course; if not, it occurred to me, I wouldn't have been surprised to see her blink the tears into the gutter, an efficient disposal system which would save her from the raking glance of Mrs Tarn. 'Anyway, Miss Harland won't be taken in,' Candida finished with a sudden note of triumph. She was running ahead to catch up with Carmen now; the gate of the Tarn home swung open, I saw, and a hand was pushing it back and forth; and at this my heart sank even further. I'd heard of the odd behaviour of Candida's brother, but had seldom glimpsed him, and could tell this was hardly a good moment to introduce a further anarchic element.

'So why won't she be taken in?' Carmen stopped, turned and stood in our way, so our passage was barred and we had to stop. This was one of her most alarming tricks, I thought with irritation: Carmen was always bringing you up against yourself, as it were, so your mind was distracted from her, her stance both moral and actual. By the time you had steadied yourself she had changed tack, or gone. 'I can tell you, Miss Carston is in on this one,' Carmen went on with her famous wide smile, taken, she told me, from Gina Lollobrigida, whom she much admired. 'So she must think it's time old Harland was taught a lesson. I mean, she doesn't want to be told her whole Art Lesson is thrown out just because an old bag is visiting the school!'

Candida's mouth was now opening and shutting gently. The green colour had gone and a faintly blue look above the collar of the Aertex games-shirt added to the impression of being in the presence of a cold-water inhabitant. It was hard to know which solecism of Carmen's had punctured the gills to this extent. Nor, of course, was it possible to know how much of Carmen's information was true and how much false. I stood there uncomfortably, watching the gate swing with an increasing rhythm and violence.

'Why you won't take anyone in,' Candida managed finally, 'is because you don't look like Lady Pickering. She's . . .' Candida searched for the word, looking Carmen up and down with hatred. Carmen was a good six inches taller, big-bosomed already and with the famous 'mass' of curly black hair which teachers tried to curb with punishment, meting out string to tie it back or, on one occasion when it covered Carmen's face in such a way that the pursuit of learning was too obviously not uppermost in her mind, condemning her to sit three full hours on a chair outside Miss Harland's room in the Main Hall, so that to pass through on the way to the Music Wing was to pass a

Medusa, the stony, grieving face lifted under a head of writhing serpents. 'She looks as if you could stand her upside down and her head was her bush,' Amy had said to me once – the type of remark which, though meaning nothing very much, gave one of those quick, surprising glimpses into Amy's way of thinking (although I didn't know at the time, of course, that Lord Lovescombe's famous collection of modern art, in which Miss Carston hoped urgently to include her brother, Sidney Carston RA, included a portrait by Magritte where this very reverse of face and genitalia was portrayed).

'Petite!' Candida had found the word which would fail to describe Carmen, but which, from the portrait in the Main Hall which we all had perforce to pass several times a day at St Peter's, would certainly apply to Lady Pickering. The tiny, almost monkey face and white silk 'tailor-made' in which she had been painted, was engraved, unwillingly in most cases, on all of us. Very thin, tiny legs in white high-heeled shoes were as delicately crossed as a ballerina's. Candida, who had often expressed her admiration for this painting of Lady Pickering, was now doubly enraged – that this elegant school governor should suffer embarrassment on Founders' Day; and that Carmen, who was endowed with pretty well everything Lady Pickering was not, should dare to present herself as this paragon of high fashion and restraint.

'Miss Carston's painting over the picture,' Carmen said with a snort of delight – at having 'got a rise' from Candida and no doubt at having walked backwards, as she had stealthily been doing since arresting our progress, arriving finally at the entrance to Candida's front garden. The gate abruptly stopped swinging. 'No one's seen Lady Pickering,' Carmen explained. 'She was only made school governor the other day. Miss Carston's going to say Lady

Pickering doesn't really look like that tiny, shrivelled thing in the portrait – she'd take offence if she saw it and all that, and Miss Carston can get hold of a really good portrait of the old girl by her brother Sidney Carston RA. How about it?' Carmen rolled her eyes. 'You'd hardly expect me to strap my legs up . . .' She took on a French accent, pulled her right leg up behind her and made a hideous Toulouse-Lautrec grimace. 'I mean, dahling, zat would be most uncomfortable!'

In the light of what happened later that evening, I was able to see that Carmen's lies could take on a far worse aspect than the Lady Pickering/Miss Carston tale, which, improbable enough to calm even Candida's apprehensions, had achieved its aim of procuring for the teller a free evening meal and a certain power over Candida, who was bound to ask Mrs Tarn in her most supplicatory tones for a special favour for Carmen, possibly even a further mattress for the night. I understood, waking suddenly with an unpleasant lurch of the heart to find myself at Love-grove, with the lamp by the far side of the four-poster still burning, left on by me from pure cowardice, that Carmen's police-interrogation methods, of throwing out misinformation and the truth together, could so baffle the hearer that a kind of instant power was achieved. I didn't know then, of course, that some of Carmen's claims were indeed true and that Lady Pickering would come in for quite a surprise the next day. We were – that is, Candida and I – so relieved by the sheer impossibility of a teacher at St Peter's joining in an idiotic prank that we lost sight of other possibilities. In any case, my thoughts were diverted at that point by a tall, dark-browed figure coming out from behind the wall of box hedge. Carmen had almost stepped back on to him and he swung the gate shut with a deliberate rudeness, as if to keep out anything to do with his sister. 'Leopold! Stop it!' Candida said.

There must have been some kind of midsummer madness in the air – it was mid-June, a cloud of dust flew up off the box hedge and a bush of white syringa in the next door garden gave off a smell suggesting late hours, parties intoxicating by their inaccessibility, white flowers in the hair of young girls – for Carmen soon had us all obeying her commands, waiting for the word that would send us off to the wild-thyme-blown banks of Regent's Park. She had something of the look, that night, of what my Aunt Babs' unsuccessful admirer, the Brigadier, would have called a 'Bolshie' Titania, painted by Richard Dadd, perhaps, in his fairyworld of fantasy: I remember thinking her eyes more than usually large and black and her cheeks were bulbous, as if she were chewing on some arcane root. Leopold, Candida's brother, certainly seemed ready to fall in with Carmen's plans. Leaving the swinging gate to its own devices he followed her to the door with a moonstruck look – the first such look I was conscious of noticing – and so suffered that other kind of pang, the pang of jealousy before there is even desire. Candida, thoroughly bad-tempered by now, pushed a stubby leg in an ankle sock up against the gate and went up the path to dump her satchel on the step. Mrs Tarn gazed out at us a moment from a lace-curtained window before coming to the door to let us in. In her hand was an apple strudel, which gave off an aroma of mulched apple and cloves.

'So you are bringing the school back to our home,' Mrs Tarn said. In her tone was considerable enmity: knowing that I at least was expected, I looked anxiously at Carmen for the apology, the graceful taking of leave. Carmen, of course, had no such intention.

'It's OK, Ma.' Leopold spoke up in a voice that was

touchingly gruff: or so I thought, in my sudden and quite unanticipated need to attach myself to an object of affection on this midsummer night. I suppose this need was something to do with wanting to be caught up in the web Carmen had spun round her, so that to vie for the attentions of this clumsy, gangling – and gangle poor Leopold did, tripping twice over his sister's satchel on the way into the hall – boy was the most clearly marked path to the adult future. Leopold's eyebrows met in the middle, as if a sooty hand had made a perfunctory smudge and moved on. I took in all this, and felt reverence.

'We're going to a dance later this evening,' Carmen said to Mrs Tarn. 'So Candida said I could come here for a bite first.'

Mrs Tarn, whether activated further in her suspicions by this talk of a 'bite' – Carmen was taller and altogether more substantial than she was, I noticed – or simply bemused by the idea of a dance (neither she nor Dr Tarn ever went out, I knew, as both were studying for extra exams, for admission to higher echelons of their professions), responded to Carmen's extraordinary statement by standing back against the wall to let us troop by. The strudel hung in her hand like a custard pie the clown has failed to throw in time.

The hall was narrow and linoleum covered. Leopold's heavy shoes sounded like a battalion coming down into the kitchen after us. Despite the summer lightness, an overhead bulb in a green shade hung over the kitchen table, which was spread with plates of black bread and a dish of hard-boiled eggs. Sauerkraut and coleslaw were in high-sided glass dishes and in a pan on a mat were frankfurters, steaming. I was to remember all this when Amy talked at Lovegrove about her teas at Candida's, and to hear the same tone, a blend of superiority and unconscious anti-

Semitism, when Amalia Drifton, making Amy repeat for the amusement of the guests at Lovegrove, the menu at the Tarns, the impossibly comic German food, laughed and waved a pale hand in pleasure at the mere sound of these alien comestibles.

Candida, used as she was to her own fare, paid little or no attention to the prepared meal. As Mrs Tarn went angrily past and into a dim scullery behind the kitchen, Candida with a quick movement pushed Carmen back out into the hall again. I half followed, intent on not being left out of any conspiracy going. Candida, however, was if anything even more angry than her mother.

'What dance?' I had never seen Candida like this: rage appeared to magnify her jaw, so that her other features diminished, leaving a picture of a rim of thick bone over a short, thick neck. 'Amy's dance, of course.' Carmen, still chewing on the invisible cud, gave a provocative laugh. 'Or Ludo's rather. It's his eighteenth.'

Candida, too clenched to emulate any masticatory movement, stared at Carmen like a bulldog faced by a rat. In the doorway just behind me hung Leopold. His breath came uncomfortably close to my neck. 'But we haven't been *asked*!' Candida said. A whole calendar of disappointments, of the night that would have been spent in the 'mansion' (as Candida insisted on calling it) in Primrose Hill; the subsequent cancellation and brave acceptance of a world in which such things can and will always happen must have made the spectacle of the boiled eggs and sauerkraut, so familiar, so unlike the fairy feast imagined at the Lovescombes' ball, particularly unpalatable. Indignation that Carmen should take her idol Amy in vain, even mention the name of a sacred brother unknown to her brought a tremor to a voice normally clipped and controlled. 'I was asked ages ago,' Carmen said. Her black eyes shone down at us. 'Ludo Lovescombe asked me, actually.'

'Rudd!' Candida said, as if uttering a response learned by heart. I remembered again her scorn on one of the windless, grey days in the games field when I had spoken of Amy and her parents as Mr and Mrs Rudd (I don't know why, probably a polite question to give Candida the impression of a shared interest in the endlessly fascinating Amy), and I'd been turned on as if I'd suddenly referred to the Head by a cheeky nickname. 'Lord Lovescombe's great-grandfather was a captain of industry.' Candida grimaced slightly, as if to evidence regret that the hours (presumably) spent with reference books in the school library should have come up with something so quotidian, even, in an unexciting way, nautical. 'His mother was an Azeby.' Here, I could tell, we were on safer ground. The name suggested rich quartering, white steeds riding against an azure sky. 'Castle Azeby in Cumbria,' Candida said, her voice betraying a view of a wimple, a countess in a physick-garden, doves fluttering. 'They built Lovegrove in Wiltshire as well. One of the oldest families in England. And very much to the fore in politics in the second half of the last century.'

As far as I recall, I yawned in Candida's face, history being one of the subjects that most bored me at St Peter's. To have to hear about Norman keeps and the Victorian politics while out on the games field seemed altogether to be going too far. Now, as we still stood pressed in the entrance to the kitchen, murky despite the summer day (or because of it, perhaps: a weed-choked back-garden next door overshadowed the low room with grass that had turned already to hay, and elder trees with a burst of nodding faces, ruffed by deep green leaves), Candida, after her explosion of 'Rudd!' fell silent. Carmen's lies were of course well-known to her. But – I saw Candida struggling with the implications – there was something oddly convincing about Carmen's claim to have been invited. It was wishful thinking, no doubt, that it might be possible to go to the ball, but it was midsummer; one could almost feel Candida's dream of the open sward, the ball, the music and the wafting scent of roses from Queen Mary's garden (described by Candida on previous occasions as a perfect place to wander with Amy before it was time to go in to the 'mansion' for tea). Carmen, aware of the web of illusions she had created, gave another laugh. I felt Leopold stiffen behind me. Mrs Tarn emerged from the scullery with a rosette of cold meats on a plate and we turned guiltily, the dish in itself serving as a reproach for an extra guest, unwanted.

'Ludo told me to bring you – and anyone else I liked,' Carmen said. 'He knows his parents think Amy's too young for the ball and they stopped her asking her best friend.' Fatally, compassion had entered Carmen's voice. I saw Candida blinking back tears. 'He says he thinks that's very unfair. There's going to be a marquee.'

Before I had time to wonder whether Carmen, the anarchist and gypsy, had fallen prey to Candida's disease and was hoping to meet or possibly ensnare a Spanish grandee or a French moustachioed marquis or the like, Mrs Tarn barked out an order from behind us. 'Sit! Eat!' (I was always to think of her in terms of these orders; and of a pointing finger oddly jagged in appearance – as if it could by itself cut or slice – with which she would indicate the item on the table that she wanted passed down to her.) There was time, however, for Leopold, seeing the look of anguish and indecision on his sister's face, to put in a word, earn the first hint of scornful gratitude from Carmen, who had by now completely entranced him.

'Martin next door's got a car,' he said. 'We can go in that.' Seventeen, an unimaginably remote age, presented itself. That Leopold actually had a driving licence, like American kids in the films just coming over the Atlantic with their depiction of Cadillacs and double dates, was highly impressive. Carmen nodded disdainfully.

'Sit! Eat!' said Mrs Tarn.

CHAPTER EIGHT

It seemed to me on that night at Lovegrove, when I had to rise to pull back the thick velvet curtains – it was hot and airless in the room – that Mrs Tarn had put up less protest than expected at the prospect of our going to the ball. She was unaware that we'd be going as gatecrashers, of course; but Candida's tales of the 'drunk man' to be found at the Lovescombes (presumably poor Victor Crane, as I now saw) would surely have put a responsible mother on her guard. Mrs Tarn was highly responsible, but caught like her daughter in the vision of England as represented by the Lovescombes. Neither she nor Dr Tarn, she was correct in seeing, would be guests at any of the great houses studied by their daughter with such gusto: Candida, however, with her fair, fine skin and perfect mastery of English should have the chance of going out in society, marrying into it even, if they permitted themselves to think that far ahead. (For them, indeed, Candida's maturity was near achievement, for they lacked that sense of an infinitely protracted childhood especially beloved by the English – and in particular by Amy's family, as I was so painfully to discover.) It was that evening that I saw Candida, I think for the first time, as a woman and not as a girl, as I, for example, was certainly encouraged to remain for at least the next three or four years by my Aunt Babs, whose drawings of the schoolgirls of the past hung in my bedroom, Holland smocks, Tam O'Shanters and all. It was Mrs Tarn's way of seeing the evening ahead which affected me, I suppose: even Carmen, who had always appeared a Bacchante (tearing her male prey to pieces with her bare hands on nights of Dionysian orgies, riding the centaurs in the groves), seemed comparatively innocent beside the mask of Central European complicity adopted at the tea-table by Mrs Tarn and Candida. Leopold, clearly unaware of all this, sat with his gaze still fixed on Carmen. He was humbly wretched by now, the young votary due to be sacrificed at the solstice in order that the Queen shall reign for another year. Now and again his gaze moved over to me, as if seeking some relief in a banal object.

'You can wear the black sequin,' Mrs Tarn said.

Candida looked back at her with clouded eyes. It was a religious moment. I imagined the black sequin dress gliding across the dance floors of Vienna with Dr Tarn and then leaving in a night train, securely packed in a box on the rack for England. I wondered if there was a fur stole: there was. 'You can take the fox,' Mrs Tarn said.

In the silence which ensued I realized I had to go back to Aunt Babs'. A collective madness had settled on the table in the small house off Shepherd's Bush: the weeds in the back-garden next door had turned to fairy footmen, the pumpkin-turned-carriage was about to roll to the door. I – and only I, it seemed – was perfectly sure Carmen had not been asked to the ball. How would she know Amy's brother, anyway? What would happen to us if we set off in the car belonging to the boy next door, parked near the zoo where, Amy told me, the lions roared at night and kept her awake, and were then refused admission at the door? It was unbearable to consider it. Besides, as the talk of the 'black sequin' made plain to me, I had nothing to wear.

'There are some dresses here,' Candida said in a grand tone, seeing my discomfort and succeeding in increasing it at the same time, a trait which was to prove invaluable to her in later years. 'That'd be all right, wouldn't it, Mummy?'

'Mummy' being – or so I have always thought – an intensely whimsical and over-English word, I shrank again and said I should get home and ask Aunt Babs first. 'Mummy' had shown a sudden gulf between me and Candida, I think: in saying the inoffensive, awkward word she had become, paradoxically, utterly foreign to me. 'Go on, Jenny,' Carmen said. With large, ink-stained fingers she pulled the shell off a hard-boiled egg. 'I'm going like this. Ludo said he didn't mind.' We all goggled as Carmen pulled down the shoulders of her St Peter's tunic to reveal what looked like the top of a black-silk 'slip'. For the first time since she had entered into the fantasy of the ball with Candida, Mrs Tarn looked doubtful. 'It's just a joke,' Carmen said. She laughed heartily, pushing hard-boiled egg into her mouth. Leopold stared with a helpless desperation at the straps of the black slip and Carmen's powerful upper arms. 'I brought a dress in a bag. Quite a sweet dress, really. More of a sari. The Maharanee, my aunt, gave it to me.'

Again, Mrs Tarn looked uncertain. A chasm opened up – between Candida, who was rapidly losing faith in Carmen and her pronouncements, in the validity of the invitation to the Lovescombes', in the reality of a world in which such things could be mocked – and her mother, who, feeling no doubt she had made a fool of herself in front of her daughter's friends, now regretted her credulity. The chasm, I sensed, widened as Mrs Tarn, deciding to blame Candida for having been taken in, assumed an air of high irritation at her daughter's eager acceptance of a dress for the ball. We all watched in silent embarrassment as the 'sequin' changed back to rags and the crowd of courtiers at the window to rank grass. 'The washing up,' Mrs Tarn said. 'You will now do this, Candida. Then you will revise the algebra as we have talked of earlier.'

'But –' Candida said. Her jaw was still prominent and her eyes had a puzzled, obstinate look. It occurred to me that the shock of the illusion and its riddance had been too much for her and that she was still trying to cling to the idea of dressing up for a midsummer-night's masquerade.

'The ball –' Carmen said, in a tone suggesting she was only being helpful.

A door opened at the front of the house, signalling the return of Dr Tarn. We listened to a case going down slap on the linoleum and a raincoat being shrugged off. For some reason a hush fell over the table. Leopold, who had gone a deep crimson, rose to leave the room.

'The ball –' Carmen said again, this time definitely impudent. 'You are hardly going to keep your poor little Candida at home, Mrs Tarn?'

I have to admit that Carmen's 'pure bloody cheek' as Aunt Babs' luckily infrequent visitor, the regimental suitor, would have put it, made me understand what it is to say that something 'took one's breath away'. The slight German accent which Carmen had slipped into her voice made the whole thing about as insulting as it would be possible to imagine. Despite myself I couldn't resist looking up at Leopold, who stood above us like an unsure, even crumbling, fortification. He had heard his mother made fun of: the full Oedipal significance of this dimly dawned on me. And insulted by the woman with whom he had just fallen in love. A deep purple still, he loomed over the plates of blood-sausage and pumpernickel. Mrs Tarn gave a groan of rage. I lowered my eyes, no longer able to bear Leopold's abject state. I was afraid, too – Carmen had unleashed a violence in the Tarn household: the household gods had been taken in vain. Mrs Tarn's serrated finger shot out, her face dark now, a more dangerous colour than her son's. 'Leopold!'

I felt Candida shrink at the rasping tones. Was her mother about to instruct her brother to throw Carmen out of the house? To horsewhip her even (a memory of such terms being supplied, as were the others, by the Brigadier)? Leopold was certainly the only one among us with the capacity to tackle Carmen, though the command might prove unacceptable to him in his present condition. I prayed that the whole scene would magically remove itself, the best thing about this particular midsummer's dream, as far as I was concerned, being the waking up from it. But, as so often with fervent hopes, this was not to be granted. Mrs Tarn, having taken my downcast expression for a sign of insubordination, rapped loudly on the table. 'Jenny! You will take the plates with Candida and you will wash them.' The voice had become louder and more grating: Candida and I rose and began to clear the plates. 'Leopold, you will take this to your father!' A slice of the strudel was placed on a plate. This was followed by a glass of milk. We all watched as if our lives depended on it. 'Carmen!' Neither Candida nor I had the courage to stay in the room at this point. Candida, with a dangerously high stack of plates, made for the scullery. Bearing the platter of untouched meats, some of which had taken on the greyish-purple tinge of their owner, I followed her. An ancient sink in the scullery stood in front of a window open onto the tangled garden. Candida turned on the tap, which gave a loud gush. A packet of soapflakes stood empty on the sill. 'Never mind.' Candida frowned, pushing the plates under the cold water. 'It'll be all right like this.'

I became aware then, I think, of both Candida's vulnerability and her extraordinary determination to overcome it. I was impressed by the controlled, careful scrubbing of the plates and by a sense, hard to describe, of Candida's resolution undergoing the utmost test, her character, like that of a child in a fairytale, developing with seven-league strides. I wasn't prepared, though, for so great a transformation as when, turning to me (I had been given a towel and was drying the plates, a task terrifying enough at that time, for I knew, with nightmare prescience, that I would drop one and the scullery floor was made of stone), Candida said: 'Very well, Jenny. We shall go!'

'What?' I juggled with Mrs Tarn's key-pattern plate, and Candida caught it as it slipped from my fingers. Her presence of mind and calm made her words, coming from one for whom 'getting into trouble' at school would mean prolonged punishment from Dr and Mrs Tarn and who was herself, as was well known, a rigid follower of discipline and tradition, all the more alarming.

'After everyone's gone to bed,' Candida said in a low, guttural tone, cold water from the tap splashing over her voice, thus making her purposely inaudible, I realized, to Mrs Tarn next door. My heart gave a slight, faint slide. 'We will go to the ball.' Candida looked surprised by her own words, but she didn't retract them. We stood there in the poky little back-room and stared at each other. Candida had taken it for granted that I would do what she said. And I suppose, somewhere under the dream of the Lovescombe ball that had pervaded all our minds and then faded to cobwebs, the allure was still too powerful to resist. The night was certainly young: it was impossible to imagine revision of algebra followed by the camp bed in Candida's room and the creaking of lino as Dr Tarn, worn out from his evening's work, came up to bed. The night rushed towards us, as black sequin-spangled as Candida would have been if Carmen hadn't shattered the dream for us. In the arms of the night lay marquees clouded with white netting; gold chairs, geraniums, strawberries. 'Let's get our algebra done,' Candida said, in a loud, matter-of-fact voice. I saw she had turned off the tap before saying this. 'I think we should put in double-time tonight.'

So it was that the evening, laid out on the rails of illicit promise, stretched before us into night. We went into the dining-room, where Mrs Tarn, the oilcloth on the table shining frenziedly, was engaged in darning her husband's grey socks. We stood and watched a moment, as the needle darted in and out at the head of the mushroom. Mrs Tarn failed to look up. Carmen had finally made her departure. Leopold also was nowhere to be seen. A vague thumping from upstairs suggested he had gone back to his room, where he spent most of his time, I knew, and from which he would issue orders for food by banging on the floor with a broomstick.

'We'll do our revision next door,' Candida said. (I had realized on my last visit that, despite Dr Tarn's being interrupted at his own studies if the sitting-room was used by us, this was considered preferable to our being in Candida's bedroom, where we could reasonably be expected not to revise.) 'Jenny,' Candida went on, slightly desperate now, I thought, for the attention and approval of her mother, 'did you bring the exam paper? I did.'

I said I hadn't, thus emphasizing, I felt, the efficiency of the Tarn household and its attitude to scholastic endeavour compared to my Aunt Babs' way of bringing me up, which Candida had once confided to me was considered 'scatty' by her parents. Mrs Tarn, as deaf none the less to her daughter's righteous tone as to Leopold's thumps from the ceiling above us, continued to thread her way in and out of the toe of the sock. Candida went with her most jerky and 'determined' walk to the door, and I went after her. Already it had become hard to believe that Carmen had ever been a visitor at the Tarns'.

If I had forgotten any scruples I might have had at Aunt Babs' reaction to my behaviour on my first night away from home, Candida had obliterated, or so it seemed, the last vestiges of moral obligation to her parents. We dressed with a martial punctiliousness – dictated by Candida, of course – in strange, musty-smelling dresses rescued from mothballs and shrouds: Mrs Tarn's relics from happier days in the Weimar Republic. There was no sign of the black sequin, which came as something of a relief: to have gone to the ball glittering with a stolen brightness would surely have been tempting providence. Candida said we would wear school coats; I was grateful too, that the fox, its fangs perilously close to my hand as I searched the bags for the dress I was instructed to find, was thought too ostentatious. I failed to understand, however, though I took its necessity as calmly as I did all Candida's decisions, why the wearing of her school hat was considered mandatory. I was too relieved, at the time, perhaps, not to be told I was expected to wear mine. Later on, wondering why I had accepted the inevitability of this strange compulsion on her part, I came to think that it must have summed up the many strands – contradictions, as Leopold was at that time learning to call everything that came his way, in his first flush of Marxism – in Candida's personality. The hat identified the school of which she was so proud, while at the same time, if she were caught wearing it at a late hour in a

London street on the way to gatecrash a distant party, its presence on her head would bring disgrace to that institution, with its wealth of invented traditions, from which she felt, however hard she might try to belong, excluded. The gesture, I was also to see, cried out for attention – even arrest – as if the disobedience to her parents, as terrible and unthinkable a thing as treachery to the school, could hardly go unpunished for long. It was a symbol, too, of Candida's love for Amy that she would go to such lengths to rescue her (for this was, no doubt, Candida's way of seeing the expedition: I don't think she had any idea of finding romance or glamour for herself). Carmen had described a lonely figure at an upper window, denied her 'best friend' while her family and brother danced and wined; and Candida would climb, as she must have perceived it, at least metaphorically, up the rope of hair let down to her by Amy from that high casement.

As for my own role in this expedition, it would be hard to say what my hidden motives could be. The decision was more frightening now that Carmen and her portable dream-factory had gone: there was only a stifling, rather dull feeling of fear, punctuated by the snores of Dr Tarn in the next room and the odd, inexplicable thump from the landing bedroom, as if Leopold, avid for food and service even in his sleep, had reached for the broom handle and tapped out his command. Otherwise, there was little time for reflection. Candida had by now set her hat firmly on her head, pulled the elastic under her chin which, accentuated in this way, took on a life of its own, appearing to lead us both out of the room and down the stairs. We went as quietly as was possible over the lumpy lino down the hall, drew back the chain (which was, I think for Candida, the most painful reminder of the subversiveness of her act), and walked out into the front garden and the ill-lit street, with its smell of dog's pee and box.

Even in this deliberately 'naughty' behaviour Candida was, as it seemed to me then, remarkably direct and unswerving in her loyalty to Amy. What Candida had decided on was 'childish', certainly, but Amy's own brand of childishness was of a more perverse kind. Amy was capable, as I was one of the few to witness, of involving another person in a dangerous situation because it seemed to her amusing. The incident at St Peter's concerning the impersonation of Lady Pickering was to make that clear the next day. (For it was Amy who, dressed as a maid, announced the preposterously garbed Carmen, at the door of the Head's office, as Lady Pickering; only to send her sprawling as I, passing by alone at the time was able to see, with a well-aimed kick, which had a sort of double effect, Miss Harland then falling under the impact of Carmen.)

However all that may be, our walk through the silent streets to Regent's Park was fated to be a brief one. Candida's hat, moving with lunar serenity just ahead of me, attracted a police officer as we were half-way down Holland Park Avenue. Like an early martyr, Candida looked up into the eyes of the 'arm of the law' without flinching. And, the usual questions having been asked and answered, we found ourselves accompanied back to the Tarns' house in a police car. That a PC was stationed all night outside (to prevent our flight into prostitution, presumably) may have accounted for the treatment meted out to Candida by Dr Tarn, for after we had come in, and the constable, depositing us, had gone off despite Dr Tarn's assurances that he would keep us under lock and key, to stand under a lamp-post by the neighbours' house, I was shown to a small room, a sort of box-room where towels and a large filing cabinet were pushed aside to make way for the camp bed I had previously occupied in Candida's room, while Candida was 'seen to' there by Dr Tarn. I heard the whack of what sounded like a slipper coming down through Mrs Tarn's old dress onto Candida and then the kiss of key in lock as Dr Tarn imprisoned his daughter for the night.

Two days later we stood on the asphalt in the playground just outside the science block. Girls, and an occasional mistress, passed by in white lab-coats. It seemed almost incredible that two major turning-points in our lives had taken place within the last twenty-four hours: the first being, of course, the disobedience of Candida to her parents and an attempted flight into evil, as our venture was regarded; the second being the expulsion of Carmen the day before, immediately after the Governors'-Day prank. It was nearly time to go home: to my deep humiliation I was to be 'met' at the school gates by Aunt Babs, who, having been apprised by the Tarns of my wilful and illicit behaviour, had announced she would escort me home from school every day, as if I were a five-year-old. Any complaints would result in my parents being informed and my inevitable removal to boarding-school. The day, apart from its anticipated unwelcome ending, had been uneventful, the impersonation of Lady Pickering, like a crime air-brushed out of history, seeming to belong to a distant past. Only Candida, whose face was whiter than usual, with blue veins standing out on her neck at the base of a jaw now so squared with tension that it was impossible not to see a permanent elastic-line under the chin, holding it in place, betrayed the nervous shock of the preceding nights and days. Her arms, unusually long, swung either side of her gym-slip as if she were limbering up to take the next blow: the worst part of it being that the blow might come from anywhere, including herself. For Candida had discovered, in her treachery to her parents, a new uncertainty, and the athletic, over-long arms went to and fro in a pendulum of readiness. She was, I could see, both frightened and prepared.

'Isn't it awful?' Amy, cause – or catalyst at least – of all this trouble, came up with that quick, silent walk so many of the girls made fools of themselves in copying. Her hair was tied back with a piece of string, I saw; and this gave her an innocent, perplexed look, as if the screwing back of the hair had given her forehead lines of thought and consideration. 'They're really on the war-path,' she explained, tugging at the string. 'Said my hair was getting in my eyes. "Go to the art-room and get it tied back with string!" ' Amy's imitations of staff members were famous, but today no one laughed. A small band of girls looked with sympathy at Amy as they went by. Candida blushed at this act of desecration. 'So Miss Carston had to tie me up.' We both (Candida and I, that is, Amy had turned to wave to another bunch of younger admirers) stood silently envisaging Miss Carston stooping over Amy's head, per-haps taking the opportunity to suggest once more the inclusion of a Sidney Carston RA in Lord Lovescombe's collection of modern art.

'How was the ball the other night, Amy?' Candida said. I knew she would never tell Amy of our outing and its humbling consequences, and resolved to keep quiet on the subject myself, but this proved hard when Amy burst out laughing and said that: 'Something certainly must have come over Carmen in the last day or two. Do you know, my parents had to call the police?'

Candida went, if possible, even paler. I thought of her suddenly with pity, imagining her walks in Queen Mary's rose-garden with Amy, her vulnerability to anything Amy could say or do to her. Not for the first time, I wondered just how much Amy knew of her power; and, still at that point uninfected by the blind love, infatuation even, for her that I was nearly to fall prey to in my time, I felt the chill of dislike again, as I had on that day in the art-room, the day of the sneeze and the trouble it had brought to everyone except Amy. 'Carmen suddenly arrived at the ball. In the marquee. She had on huge brass curtain-rings. She's had her ears pierced, of course.'

I knew this was a great preoccupation of Amy's, that she wasn't allowed to have her ears pierced, 'like the other girls', though in fact it was only Carmen, guardian-less as we felt she must be, who had walked the school with two festering wounds in her earlobes for days, these then being filled by small gold hoops given her, or so she claimed, by a French film-star.

'But were you allowed to – to be at it?' Candida asked. Her jaw seemed to swallow her words, burying them back in her throat before they could get up for air.

'Oh yes. Mummy always says one thing and means another. She wasn't too pleased, though, when she saw Carmen, I can tell you.' Amy laughed, then, seeing herself suddenly as less than attractive, perhaps, pulled the string off her head altogether. A fine wash of pale brown hair fell over her face. Candida fought rising and submerging words, as her neck thickened like a boa constrictor's. The Rapunzel fantasy was clearly fading fast; and there was mention of the police, too, to contend with. It must have been painful for Candida to look back on our fiasco of two nights before while remembering the sturdy back of the constable under the Tarns' neighbours' lamp.

'Why the police?' Candida said at last. Amy, however, had clearly an even more arresting picture to recount. She came right up close to us, so that we seemed to be exchanging the most conspiratorial of words: a biology teacher in a white overall and carrying a bunch of files, passed us and threw us an enquiring look. A first-year girl sped over the asphalt towards us and I drew back, sensing that a junior had been sent to fetch me: my Aunt Babs, I felt sure, was on the pavement outside the gates of the school.

'It's Miss Harland,' Amy said. Her voice was so full of enjoyment that poor Candida desperately tried to join in the laughter. 'A Head of school who wears pink silk knickers,' Amy said. 'I just had to find out. When Carmen tripped her up –'

'But, Amy, you shouldn't have done that!' Candida said. I must say I admired her for the effort of refusing to join the laughter, in which there was a ring of love for the cruel and the ridiculous. 'Carmen's been expelled, did you know?'

Something in me sank as Candida said that: I knew somehow that Amy did know. 'Oh yes, but she absolutely hated it here,' Amy said, looking put out a moment at this.

'But what's going to *happen* to her?' Candida said, anguish making her almost incoherent. 'I mean, she'll get such a –'

The words went unsaid, partly because the junior had arrived with the information that my Aunt Babs was indeed at the main gate and would I come quickly please: and partly, I suspect, because the memory of Dr Tarn's slipper as punishment was still too fresh. Images of the Head's pink-knickered state also, as such images will, imposed themselves on all our minds. It was a part of Amy's fatal charm, I think, that she could mix the absurd and the ordinary so effortlessly. Now she turned to me with a look of astonishment. 'Come to pick you up? Your Aunt Babs? No, I'll tell you why the police were called to the ball. Carmen came with some joke figure who parked his Morris

Minor right up against the princess's car. The Morris Minor – and the driver who had no business to be there in the first place – both had to be towed away!'

Even to think of these humiliations for Candida – or to half-dream, half-remember them in the depths of the great four-poster at Lovegrove – was to bring an unease which woke me at dawn, to hear the sound of sheep in a meadow the other side of the river, this revealing itself on looking out through heavy silk curtains at the River Love full and grey, with meadows and runnels of silver water lying along them like metal strips binding them in. Even the sheep here, it didn't surprise me to see, were strange in appearance, like nothing in the Hertfordshire fields where my parents had briefly farmed before going overseas, the horns forming an exotic calligraphy along the lines of water, and finally executing a kind of arabesque as they interlocked and re-formed in half-moons again. Their coats, brown and white and thick, added a note of tapestry to the scene; and I half expected a garland of roses to appear in the dull green of the field, or to reach out and discover the sheep's fleece was in fact brown canvas, the picture wearing thin before dissolving with the mists of early morning.

A watery sun rose. I don't know what made me decide then to wander out of the house, to cross the slender bridges over the 'cuts' in the garden and walk in the meadows – a desire to be free, perhaps, of the long night's dreams and exacerbations, the puzzlement of dinner the night before, and earlier of Amy seen for the first time as painfully sensitive to the behaviour and reactions of her parents: a new Amy, tentative, unhappy, even afraid. I thought too, I believe, that I would solve some of the problems set by the power of the Lovescombe family, the power over Amy (and, too, while I was imprisoned there, over me), if I stood back from the house; crossed the river and saw it, as it were, as 'just a house', escaped the deadly glamour the place seemed to exert over both those born to it and those strangers foolish enough to stay under the roof. I had no wish to come across Walter Neet on my way, it was true, but I tried to calm myself with the thought that Neet, for one, must see Lovegrove as 'just a house', for he was always sketching one great place or another – he simply charged his commission and enjoyed the comfort of the visit, then moved on. Something in me knew that this wasn't the case of course: that Lovegrove was 'magical' even to him, and that to stray into his path at an early hour of the morning would be dangerous, Neet being likely to consider that an apparition of a maiden in the labyrinths of Lovegrove was a gift not to be ignored. But my need to leave the tentacles of honeysuckle on the walls of my room – tentacles which, like the memories of Candida and Carmen, pulled at my thoughts and made me half-asleep and half-awake at the same time, so that I could no longer tell to which world I belonged – was greater than the fear of meeting Neet. I pulled on a sweater over pyjamas bought by Aunt Babs in Edinburgh on a visit two years before (and therefore embarrassingly short in the leg and arm); put my feet into black gym-shoes, and left the room.

The passage, with its ornate carpet stretching out in its pattern of red and white and grey like a trail from the shot game with which Lovegrove decorated its entrance, ended at a door of some light wood, cedar perhaps, with a stiff door handle, wedge-shaped and of brass. I leant down on its coldness, my heart beating at the silence of the house, a silence deeper than the before-dinner hush, a silence given over to the portraits in the Old Drawing-Room and on the walls of the passage itself, which in their own stillness had an unpleasant air of being about to shout. The door opened as noiselessly as all else, on to a total blackness. Yet it was dawn, day even, in the water-meadows; I was only to reflect later that the 'back stairs' in houses such as Lovegrove were built to be as black as pitch both day and night, whether to encourage the fast run of chambermaids in the dim light of the first electricity, or to deter bachelors, historically placed in these dim quarters, to stay put and not to roam in the direction of the ladies, I did not know.

My reason for all this – for avoiding going down the main stairs – was, I'm sure, the oppressive presence of the portraits: in particular, at the top of the great staircase down into the Hall, a man with black hair, one of the 'black Azebys', as I had heard Neet refer to this mysterious branch of the family. Beside this menacing figure sat a woman in a pose of humility: white mobcap, folded hands. The light had indeed come into the main hall and fell from the high windows straight on to them. And something in the dark gazer's eye made me think of his descendant, Lord Lovescombe; to hear distant morning gongs and see him creep from Jasmine Tremlett's room – and surely, as I told myself, in panic, I would suffer the consequences if I were to catch him *in flagrante delicto* twice in one night: in the worst of possible taste, in fact. The house gave a long, creaking shudder as I stood at the door to the back stairs. The footsteps of maids seemed to run in the shudder, the sound of the starting up of an Edwardian morning, with ewers of water and hip-baths painted round with geese and duck in beds of reeds. The patter of returning lovers, long dead, eyeless now as they had once been circumspect, seemed to come up on the air from all the closed doors, doors still named with the innocent, floral names of those summers of betrayal and deceit.

There was nothing to guide me but the need to go down rather than back – and the rough edges of the carpet, haircord in this part of the house, which led me on. I clung to the banisters and stared at a blackness so dense that green circles, like the 'after-light' that comes from staring at the sun, came up in front of my eyes. Somewhere, deep down, someone must stir, make a cup of tea, grumble about the lack of kippers or the hens not laying right. But there was no kitchen sound or smell: the house was like a giant doll's house where the plaster food, once served by the children, is tidied away into a cupboard until the next game.

I dare say, if I'd known then what I was later – half at least – to know, I would not have been surprised by such thoughts of children and their games on the back staircase at Lovegrove. I would have been able to recognize in myself too a longing for the sort of gilded childhood both Amy and her brother enjoyed (so unlike that of Candida and the unfortunate Leopold, the image of whom, towed away from the Lovescombe ball, by a police vehicle in the borrowed secondhand car, had given an almost unbearable source of pain and embarrassment to Candida and, it may be said, a certain amount to me); a childhood I was seeing just as we were all leaving it.

In the deep well of the stairs, when I had gone down and down, feeling the bumps of the painted wall under the palms of my hands, a faint light gleamed. It showed the passage, painted half a century before in a green deemed suitable for pain, servitude and penniless younger sons: the green of a back stairs of the plutocracy who must needs keep their inferiors in check; a green of raw apples far removed from the scenes of gluttony on the other side of the deeper-green baize door. The haircord carpet, revealed in this light to be a prison grey, turned up some steps and marched down a short corridor: the lamp, a frosted-white bluebell with curlicues on the glass, hung in the high green shoebox of a passage that led nowhere, allowing two rooms

110

to feed off it to right and left, neither door in this case with a card-holder or name.

The far door was open. The room had been a schoolroom once, probably, for the books in the bookshelves had a shabby, used air, unlike the unread leather volumes in the drawing-room. There was a maple table with a claw-foot and a battered white sofa. The room could be 'placed' further by noting the curtains, of which I could see, from my angle of imminent flight, only a fold or two: red, of a cheapish stuff too 'serviceable' to replace; chosen, probably, to suit the occupants of the room: children, the children of guests, a tutor or governess. Framed prints of the seasons of the year hung about the walls. At that time I saw only a woman in a frilly lace head-dress holding a sheaf of wheat: August, I think. She looked out over the back of the stubby little sofa on which Ludo sat, his long fair hair falling, as Amy's so often did, over his face. A girl, almost obscured from sight by Ludo's back and encircling arm, lay against him. A pair of satin pumps, just becoming fashionable at the time and dyed a deep strawberry pink, lay by the unused grate.

I can't say that I retreated quietly or with diplomacy. The surprise – the shock, even – of the strength of my reaction on seeing Ludo kissing 'another' (so fast is the sexual awakening of the mind at that age) was so powerful that I walked backwards into a slab of green wall and bounced off it to come back painfully at the facing wall in the narrow corridor. Ludo looked up and out at me. His eyes had a drowned, blue gaze as if he had really 'come up for air' (as Carmen used graphically to describe her kissing sessions with her latest boyfriend) and I pictured, fleetingly, a deep-sea diver, down at the bottom of an immensely deep and pitch-black stairwell, fighting his way up in a dome of glass to the light at the top. The girl made no movement. 'Jenny,'

111

Ludo said, in a voice so soft it was possible he hadn't spoken at all, that what I heard were the first stirrings of the morning which had indeed finally begun in the unfathomable quarters below. 'Jenny, go back to bed.'

I went, flying down the steps at the end of the truncated corridor: down to a long dark landing where a wide door now stood ajar and the other green, the Elysian green of the carpets of the Lords of Lovegrove stretched out for those with the means to walk on them. And I ran, as if in a game for which the rules have long been forgotten, across the bright expanse of the great hall and up the wide staircase to 'my' room.

CHAPTER NINE

It was bright morning. Amy was sitting on the end of my bed. Through the curtains of the four-poster came the same sound of sheep bleating, but slower and deeper, as if the sun and the lines of bright water had closed them in and given them angles of being, a perspective for the day. The dreams of the night seemed further off than the beasts: dark, twisted, forgotten. I could hardly tell what I had seen and what I hadn't; clearer than the penumbrous descent to Ludo's 'bachelor' quarters was the vision of Candida, arms folded outside the red brick of the science lab, eyes cold with longing for the end of term, the promised visit to Lovegrove. The day after that she fell ill. But I saw her, as can happen with the vividness of dream, as clearly as if it had been she who had walked down the back stairs, a shining invisible companion in the dark; she who had lain beyond reach of my gaze, in the sofa and in Ludo's arms. I sat up, rubbed the sleep from my eyes. With that sudden acceptance of things to come, of the inevitability of what is about to be said, I leant forward and smiled at Amy. She looked happy today, as if the tensions and unexplained appearances and disappearances of the night before had been blown away, flakes in a child's snowstorm.

'Candida rang. The doctor says she's well enough to

travel,' I heard Amy with that sense of the expected, the always-known but not admitted fact. I would have to withdraw into myself, I thought: Candida comes with all her worship, her determination to take over Amy – and I couldn't help thinking then of the famous jaw, of Candida the boa constrictor swallowing Amy while I looked on helpless, pretending even to be amused. I would retreat, I knew, to the world Aunt Babs had made possible for me, a world of 'looking-at-pictures', of 'mooning around' with sketchbook and HB pencil, filling in the strokes of the River Love as it flowed down to meet the River Avon at the weir. I would go and look at Lord Lovescombe's collection of modern art and tell Miss Carston more about it when I got home than Amy, bored as she was with her own family's treasures, ever could. I might, just when I thought I was alone – and here I saw it to be the Japanese paper boathouse in the middle of the fast-running brown current – find Ludo. We might sit on the odd, miniature furniture of cane and paper and look down together at the floor of water plaiting over pebbles and weed. This seemed wildly unlikely, I had to confess, and I had to stop – in time to hear Amy say: 'She doesn't come until later – Candida, I mean. Let's go in the woods, you remember, to the house – well, it's called The Far House in the Woods – where my Uncle Si lives. Shall we, Jenny?'

I said I'd get dressed. Amy said we'd have a quick breakfast, so as not to be caught by the old bores, by which I assumed she meant Walter Neet. I rose as Amy, dressed already in a kind of stable-boy's outfit of baggy old trousers, brown shirt and a sleeveless jerkin that looked as if it had been rolled several times in the mud, was making for the door of the Honeysuckle Room. She looked, I thought, in that flash which heightened emotions (even disappointment, as the news of Candida's arrival had to be) can give to the eye, like a young bucolic visitor to the chamber of the lady of the house – a lad come to call on the mistress, perhaps, in a painting by Fragonard – to break the news of the hunt gathering outside. Then she turned, pointing to the great chest of drawers at the door where I'd searched in vain for my few dresses and skirts. 'My father's great-aunt left all her hats in this once. They had to be driven at break-neck speed after her. But she was a speed-fiend herself. And she was on her way to the north of Scotland.' Amy grinned, pulling at the handle of the heavy door. 'The chauffeur had to go up as far as John o'Groats to hand her the hats. And on the way back the car overturned at Glencoe. He was killed.'

'Amy!' I said. As so often, it was impossible to tell with this story whether or not one was supposed to laugh or commiserate: the loss of a chauffeur being in all likelihood a worse consequence of the journey north – to the Loves-combes at least – than the death of a man. On the other hand, the hats were clearly thought to be funny. I decided to go on with the question which had been forming in me, for Amy; and in retrospect I do see that I wanted only assur-ance from her, assurance that I wouldn't be 'left out', as children (and later, in most cases, adults, dread to be); that Amy and Candida wouldn't disappear altogether and leave me to face alone the coolness of Lady Lovescombe and the furtive prowlings of her mate.

'I mean, is everything all right here?' I said. 'Would you rather I went home? I just felt' – and this was hard to say, I knew, after my blunder of the night before and Amy's angry reaction to it – 'I just felt that things aren't OK and maybe you'd rather I went home. I mean, the more people you have to stay, the more –'

'The more what?' Amy said in a tone that was a fair imi-tation of her mother at her most glacial.

'The more difficult it is for you to cope with what's going on,' I faltered.

'What on earth do you mean?' Amy looked with an impatient sideways glance out of the window as she spoke, as if the brightness of the day would soon fade if we went on wasting time like this. I saw in her eyes the longing for the wood, the house her grandmother had built like some kind of refuge against the grown-up world – and against questions like mine too – but I had to go on. 'Isn't it very hard – with Jasmine Tremlett?' I asked.

I knew as soon as the words were out that I shouldn't have said them. Yet, with that same feeling of knowing in advance that there is no way of averting what is about to come, I was relieved too that I was asking a 'blunt' question, facing up to reality in a world of which I knew nothing and which Amy was trying to flee. I think now that as well as wanting assurance from Amy that the difficult side of life at Lovegrove wouldn't be left to me to face on my own while she and Candida escaped into the games and fantasies of childhood, I wanted Amy to 'notice' me just once before Candida arrived and took her over entirely. With such pathetic jealousies and calls for attention are the foundations for maturity laid down.

'She's like that,' Amy said. Her voice was full of scorn. 'She's like that with everyone.' Amy pulled open the door. The mouth of the dark passage, the tunnel of the middle of the night which had led me to the back of the house, the low-slung room where Ludo lay awake on a sofa until the small hours, gave behind her. In the gloom I failed to see a figure approach.

'You mean Jasmine Tremlett is a tart,' I said. I was pleased to speak like that, I can only suppose, because Aunt Babs would never have allowed it; and I was infected already a little with the callousness of Amy's class and background; the trick of placing people in quotes, or in an absurd situation for the sake of the quick burst of laughter before the next joke.

The doorway now held a bulky figure. I can't pretend there was anything *déjà vu* about this. Still in bed, in the child's pyjamas my Aunt Babs had bought in Edinburgh, my bare feet felt the clammy chill of dread. Amy stood aside. She looked up perfectly happily into her father's face, however, as if her imported friend hadn't blasphemed in church, done the unspeakable, insulted the woman Lord Lovescombe pursued through dew and over Chinese bridges. I prayed only that Amy wouldn't slip away, leaving me with the wrath of the patriarch and adulterer.

'You girls are late for breakfast,' Lord Lovescombe said. (I was still unable to look up and face him squarely in the eye: the voice was that of the child's picturing of Big Bear tracking down the missing Goldilocks as she wanders from one bed to the next.) 'Hurry up with it, and I'll take you both down to the weir.'

He hadn't heard, I thought. But the matter was uncertain. Amy shot me a quick glance. 'We'll see you there, Daddy. We're going on a walk first.' I saw there was no mention of the house in the woods, and wondered if it was out of bounds. With the Lovescombe family and land, it was impossible not to feel that there was a secret code of territory everywhere. 'And another friend of mine is coming, later,' Amy went on. 'I'll have to be back here to meet her.'

'Another?' Lord Lovescombe said, with no interest in his tone whatsoever. 'Oh, very well. But for heaven's sake tell Mummy in time.'

'I have,' Amy said. I could tell from the teasing tone that the scare was over. Either her father had heard me and decided he had not, or he had actually missed it altogether.

'Because there's a big lunch party today,' Lord Loves-combe said. 'Bernard Ehrlich – the painter – with some friends. And that chap Mick Scupper – to value the early Gainsboroughs.'

Breakfast in the dining-room was laid out in a way that made the oddness of dinner the night before seem like an incongruous part of the half-dream that I seemed to have walked into on my arrival at Lovegrove. Newspapers on a sideboard by the door to the pantry gave a businesslike air, as if the place had been hired for a conference, or was temporarily in use as a cabinet minister's holiday retreat; food in long silver platters on a variety of hotplates removed the necessity of Vine, or of parlourmaids with falling plates; and a full sun pouring through the windows gave the sense of a bustling day started: of plans, and matters of national interest to be discussed, perhaps even a peerage or two to be negotiated in the course of a morning walk. That there were few 'walks' to go on – as was clear from the view from the wide plate-glass windows, where the intricacies of the Chinese garden forbade such a thing as a good English walk (as did the water-meadows opposite, confined as they were in their ribboning of water and with steep wooded hills behind) – in no way detracted from the general feeling of optimism and confidence. Even Victor Crane, more crumpled than an old newspaper (and certainly more crum-pled than those on the sideboard, ironed as they most likely had been early in the morning, Vine passing his steam-press over a pucker in Churchill's brow, pushing down on the latest reports of disease on the grouse moors of Scot-land), sat fairly peacefully over a plate of congealed kippers and eggs. A Woodbine burned in a saucer near him, while a silver ashtray, its centre rearing up in the form of a mermaid prepared to receive a cigarette in her arms at any time the smoker should desire a respite, went unheeded. I saw that, I think, because the beginning of an admiration for Victor Crane grew in me on that day: first at breakfast, when he sat quiet in his oblivion to the world of the Lovescombes, and later at lunch when all the guests had descended on Lovegrove and Crane was able to keep calm when a further domestic accident threatened to increase that intolerable teasing which seems (although I knew nothing about it then, of course) to grow as fast as ground elder in big country houses where there is little to do all day but bully or yawn. At the time Crane, stunned no doubt by the amount of alcohol he had consumed the night before, barely looked up when Amy and I came in. The paper he held – Vine had perhaps been sent to some distant drop-off point to get it (though whether he ironed it too was questionable) – was the *Morning Star*. The smoke from the 'Woodie', as Crane called his brand, coiled round the edges of the smudged-looking headlines. I wondered if the paper, if it had indeed been delivered, had been left out in the rain, another possibility, by a disapproving Lord Lovescombe, who had found it on the doorstep on one of his early-morning prowls. This pointless speculation apart, I was glad to recognize the paper which, though not taken by Aunt Babs, had a firm supporter in a friend of hers, Ethyl Bryant, who came to stay with us in the summer holidays, went to meetings and shouted hoarsely late into the night at Aunt Babs about the future of the Communist Party. Dreading, if not exactly disliking Ethyl Bryant, I noticed now that I felt quite homesick for her, the newspaper standing for a voice that was somehow lacking at Lovegrove.

'My dear Amy, you look just like a Swedish page-boy.' Amalia Drifton stood behind us, a cup of coffee in hand. With the calm, almost arrogant gestures of someone who has spent much of her life in such a place, she brushed past us and went to the window-seat which ran all the way under the windows and gave a good vantage point of the bamboo clump which, the previous evening, had enclosed her brother and Jasmine Tremlett. A small mahogany table (kept in the bay, I was later to discover, for house guests when the embarrassing contingency arose of thirteen having to sit down together: the less important or desirable people being placed at this small annex of a table) held Amalia's coffee cup and a large cut-crystal ashtray with a gold rim. Amalia Drifton drew on a du Maurier, its scarlet packet bright in the sun from the long windows. It seemed unlikely, I couldn't help reflecting, that a woman such as Amalia Drifton and a man such as Victor Crane could ever be found in the same room together, unless 'by marriage', and it seemed to me that the two ill-assorted characters looked as if they would shortly appear in an amateur production of *A Midsummer Night's Dream*, Amalia Drifton's diaphanous négligé prompting the idea of a malevolent fairy, complete with smoking wand.

'I gather the most awful crowd are coming to lunch,' Amy's aunt went on, oblivious apparently to the fact that Amy had shown little pleasure in being likened to a Swedish page-boy. 'Why on earth does she let it happen? Think of poor Mrs McTaggart is what I say.'

The 'she' I could only assume was Lady Lovescombe: a 'she' invested with such explosive hatred that it could only apply to a sister-in-law, and a powerful one at that. Mrs McTaggart, whom I secretly admired as I took my portion of creamy scrambled egg and added a kipper, must be the cook at Lovegrove. I wondered if Amalia Drifton's interference was welcome; or perhaps she had returned from 'the village' now the war was over, to take up her old post, and thus had known Lord Lovescombe's sister since childhood. As childhood was impossible to imagine as having been once an ingredient of Amalia Drifton, the thought stopped there.

'I mean, that ghastly man Bernard Ehrlich. He's such an appalling painter, too. Who wants to look like a carcass in a butcher's shop? Why on earth do all those perfectly good-looking young women go on posing for him? It's quite disgusting!'

Victor Crane stiffened at this, if stiffening were a word that could ever be used in connection with Crane, so innately floppy were his long limbs, while even his trunk seemed this morning to have taken on a limp, thrusting movement when he sat up, like the neck of a tired ostrich. Sit up, however, he managed to do, aligning himself against the back of the chair ('Chippendale original', as Lord Lovescombe said later, at lunch, as we stood around waiting to be told where to sit, the newly arrived art expert Mick Scupper noticeably absent). Crane looked out over his newspaper at the gauzy shape of Amalia Drifton in the far window-seat.

'Bernard Ehrlich keeps old Muriel's Colony Room going,' he announced in a voice which, while being husky from smoking, also sounded sentimental, almost nostalgic, so that pictures of Crane reclining as a possible subject for the painter, whether or not the finished result resembled a carcass of beef, came inevitably to mind. I must say, having heard the name of the famous, or rather, infamous artist a good many times at Aunt Babs', I was frightened and excited to hear he was coming to Lovegrove. I remembered Lord Lovescombe's 'modern-art collection' which I was yet to see, but which, by now, I thought of as a kind of mixture between Aladdin's cave and Bluebeard's secret room, a chamber where Lord Lovescombe's 'lady-friends' might find themselves incarcerated with the Henry Moores, John

Pipers, Keith Vaughans and Graham Sutherlands which doubtless lurked there: a place quite unsuitable for the works of Sidney Carston RA but ideal for the wilder aspects of Bernard Ehrlich. I glanced at Amy, hoping she might have some views on this. But she stood, with the distant expression which seemed to have come over her as soon as she walked through the entrance hall of Lovegrove: a glazed look, I thought then, that was not unlike the glassy stare of the stunned animals depicted there.

'I mean, it's so hopelessly inconsiderate. Why on earth she should allow it, I can't think. Just because Ehrlich goes to stay everywhere.'

This sentence needing some interpreting, I glanced at Amy again. 'She' was clearly Lady Lovescombe, showing once again her powers of mismanagement as a hostess; 'everywhere' must mean, I supposed, the 'smart' houses where Amalia Drifton would herself have liked to go. 'I wasn't here when he came the last time,' Amy said. 'Is he really evil, like Daddy says?'

An awkward silence would have fallen, had the company been less oddly made up; as it was, Victor Crane burst out laughing – which outburst brought on a terrible fit of coughing – and Amalia Drifton rose, looking impatient, as if Amy's naïve question had reminded her of how much time had been wasted already, in a morning where she had valuable things to do, although it was hard to see what these could be.

'I see Ehrlich at Muriel's pretty well every night,' Crane said, as if to banish in this way any suggestion of evil in Bernard Ehrlich. Another spasm of coughing came and went, leaving a shocked silence in the dining-room at Lovegrove, with its pristine ivory walls and pure, green view from sparkling windows; bringing instead a sense of dim clubs in Chelsea and Soho, known to me only through friends of Aunt Babs as they spoke of this (for me) unattainable Bohemia. 'He had a bit of a punch-up with old Jack Hare in Muriel's the other day. Hare seems to think Ehrlich helps himself where he likes – in this case, to the beautiful Jasmine Tremlett.'

I watched Amy go pale, then a deep red, then pale again. We had sat down at the big table, as far from Crane's 'Woodie' as possible; nevertheless, Amy recoiled as if about to be violently sick. Amalia Drifton, impervious it seemed to the moonlit flitting between her brother and Jasmine Tremlett, gave a dry, worldly laugh.

'I can't think why she has the Tremletts to stay here,' she said, referring once more I had to imagine to the unfortunate Lady Lovescombe, for whom, despite her condescension to me on the evening before, I began to feel pity. 'I mean, she must have known the Hares would come over. They always do when they're staying with Millie.'

Amy spread a slice of toast with butter, then decided against it and left it to lie on her plate. I watched it harden, and the corners curl.

'They won't go in for a bout of fisticuffs while they're here,' Victor Crane said, his laugh and cough bellowing out again. Amalia Drifton frowned at this, and with various floating movements connected with the strange garment she was wearing, made for the door. This opened first from the other side and Jasmine Tremlett came in. There was no suggestion of dressing-gown or négligé for her, or not this morning at least: the black polo-neck, pencil-thin skirt and eyes ringed with kohl suggested an imminent appearance in a 'boîte' on the Left Bank.

'Good morning,' Jasmine Tremlett said with a brightness suggesting time spent listening outside the dining-room door, a probably essential occupation for someone so closely connected to so many. 'Isn't it a heavenly day?'

These last words were delivered with what was known, I believe, in those days when people of my Aunt Babs' generation started to go to the movies, as a 'peek-a-boo' expression: lips puckered and then filling out in a ballooning kissing shape, eyes comically enlarged and provocative. Amy stared down at her plate.

'The table must be cleared soon for lunch,' Amalia Drifton remarked as she made for the door. There was a second in which the two women passed: a thin whisper, like a wind of dislike, could be heard between them, this probably occasioned by the nylon of which Amalia Drifton's négligé would almost certainly have been made up, and one of the articles of clothing sported by Jasmine Tremlett – the black pencil skirt perhaps.

Lord Lovescombe came into the dining-room. Victor Crane, I saw, buried his head deeper in the *Morning Star*. Several of the portraits on the walls, as if reminding themselves of their dependence on the present steward of Lovegrove, appeared to gaze both wistfully and demandingly at him.

Lord Lovescombe was an unprepossessing sight as he stood in the high-ceilinged, light room, its plasterwork ceiling a memorial to the elevated Utopian ideals (these in their day closer to the aspirations of Victor Crane than to our host) of William Morris and Dante Gabriel Rossetti. Lord Lovescombe's left eye, a victim (or so it occurred to me) of running into clumps of bamboo at night, had dropped down his face like a badly poached egg, blackened and slipping from its container. Moonshot pores stood out on his cheeks. The rubbery smile, first seen at dinner the night before as it wound itself round the goblet of claret or leered inanely down the table in the direction of Amy, had wandered off his face, so it seemed to be lying among folds of double chin and pull-out neck. A thin, rather worried pair of lips remained: these were clamped shut, as if afraid to open and reveal some unpleasant piece of information. 'We've the most enormous number to lunch,' Amalia Drifton announced to her brother. She still stood in the doorway, her diaphanous gown attracted this time to the door handle, which it flailed at in an attempt to achieve union. 'I thought some people were leaving today.'

The purport of this statement didn't go unnoticed, Lord Lovescombe staring helplessly at Jasmine Tremlett as his sister spoke while Amy, suffering suddenly from an attack of impatience (or so it seemed at the time; I was to see later that claustrophobia, a disease engendered by Lovegrove, was one of her chief afflictions), pushed back her chair with a violence that nearly caused it to fall over and stood up. I followed suit: the dining-room, however, refusing to release us until Amalia had finished her scene by the door. We all stood helpless, watching the sun dance over the carved centaurs in the marble of the fireplace and go on points in and out of the painting of a flat Norfolk scene behind the sideboard, giving life to the duns and yellows of an alien, wide-skyed world.

'The Hares are coming,' Amalia pressed her point home. 'And Bernard Ehrlich. With the possibility of several young women, I gather.'

The news certainly seemed explosive. I remember only thinking that the love-affairs of grown-ups – for Lord Lovescombe darted a look of terrifying ferocity at the mention of both names, his face at once autocratic and subservient, like an executioner just before the deed – particularly hard for those of my, or for that matter Amy's, age to understand or bear, the existence of love and anguish in a world before one's birth being as remote and unimaginable as life after death, a kind of hell. Amy now went to the door, her aunt having glided away at the end of her speech, and I followed her. The door closed behind the uneasy trio of Lord Lovescombe, Jasmine Tremlett and Victor Crane.

Lord Lovescombe wasn't going to let us go so easily, though, for as Amy, finger to lips as if we would both go into shrieks of laughter unless forcibly prevented, ran off down the green of the hall to the door to the front hall and final escape, her father appeared from the dining-room and shouted to us to stop. Amy froze in her tracks. For a time-less moment of horror I thought Lord Lovescombe, mad-dened by his sister's hostility to Jasmine Tremlett, was on the point of bringing up my earlier conjecture as to whether or not she might be a tart. A napkin was brandished, but all Lord Lovescombe wanted to know was if he would see us later at the weir. Amy turned and waved, her need to rid herself of her father almost too obvious to provoke com-ment. 'Yes, yes, we'll see you at the weir,' she called back to him as we fled.

CHAPTER TEN

If I had thought Amy's family 'strange', in the way a child
senses something out of the usual but can't say what it is,
this was perhaps because, having only half-left childhood
myself, I was in no mood to recognize this strangeness for
what it was: the permanent childhood of adults decked out
in the contents of a dressing-up box where the fabulous
furs are real and the great paste stones in the tiaras prove,
on closer examination, to come from the mines of South
Africa. Even the trees and plants in this exotic world were
different, had the strangeness of a hybrid: 'Things grow
here that don't grow anywhere else,' Amy said as we
walked down to one of the innumerable cuts, stared down
at the black treacle water through a tangle of Asiatic weeds;
and this was easy to believe, too, for it was as if the place
had become overheated, producing a 'micro-climate', so
that blossoms and shrubs from long-conquered territories
could thrive in the semi-tropical atmosphere.

Amy walked ahead of me; and we crossed the last stream
and walked through grass on stones set with a purposeful
whimsicality here and there in the soft-smelling hay – again
a children's game, testing ingenuity – 'Look!' Amy said,
'it's like a maze. My grandmother set down these stones.
If you keep to the left you're led to the greenhouse and the

reward is a peach, or an apricot,' and here she looked back
at me with a seriousness that left me confused; 'if you keep
to the right you find yourself in the wood. The squirrel's
way, she called it.'

For all the 'sick-making' (as Aunt Babs would have called
it) side of this, I have to confess I was as enthralled by it as
I had been since arriving at Lovegrove the evening before.
The stones, oblong and faded, sunk in the ground and
edged with a fur of emerald moss, seemed as inviting as a
sequence of carpets advertising their magic pathways
through the sky. The warmth of the sun on the smooth
stone – Amy had taken off her shoes and so had I – gave a
lazy, mystical lope to our walk. The trees thickened; we had
been drawn into the wood, as into so many, I suspected, of
Lady Azeby's games of power and love, without knowing
it. Only the pigeons, with their throaty call that seemed to
make the wood much deeper, the shadows longer on the
fallen arras of beech leaves, reminded of the sudden loss of
sunlight, of branches overhead so thick with green that
Amy's back – in the scruffy shirt she stubbornly wore
against all the pleas of her mother – was as dappled as a
zebra's. The stones, too, stopped suddenly as if to show
the game was over, or to tell us that we had been foolish to
be taken in by their promises in the first place, for they
led nowhere, we had wasted our time in childish pursuits
when the other path would have been better, and a stretch
of ground burnished with copper leaf rising and falling by
the cart-wheels of uprooted trees, lay in front of us without
indication of boundary or end.

'You'd never guess, would you?' Amy said. She had
pulled up suddenly and we stood abreast in a clearing
where the sun, let through at last, seemed to have lost
interest in the play of light and shadow and sent down a
baleful glare, shrinking the foreground with its massive

fortifications of tree roots and earth upturned from a distant titanic fall. The trees showed no hint of autumn here, but had the air of being preserved in a perpetual summer: a sort of calendar effect, glossy and dead.

I saw the roof of the little house in the unmoving leaves of the trees as one can sometimes see a face in the wallpaper, or the outline of eyes and nose in a ceiling crack. It took longer, though, to understand that we were already in the 'house': that the flagstones had been the entrance way and we had passed through a door of trees and undergrowth that had somehow (for there was now no way of seeing which direction we had come in) closed behind us. We were in the atrium of the 'house in the woods' which Lady Azeby had built for her children in that Edwardian summer when you could walk on the downs and the only sound was the lark or meadow pipit and nothing was enclosed: you could watch a hedgehog run, Amy said, from the side of the old grass road into the woods. I wondered if we had, in some way, walked up near to the old druidic circle. Lady Azeby, whether we were close to the enchanted ring or not, had certainly created one of her own. I was reluctant to admit that I was as drawn to this fanciful palace of childhood as repelled. Memories of infancy, when animals speak and witches lurk in the corners of the house, came sharply and not entirely unpleasantly back to me. I wanted, I confess, to lie in the piles of beech leaves that were the banked fires in the fireplaces of a twisted tree root, to sleep the child's sleep without memory or dread. My feet, however, appeared to be obeying the impulse to run away. Amy laughed out loud and grabbed my arm.

'Don't run, Jenny. People sometimes feel like that when they come here for the first time. Not that everyone gets brought here, I can assure you!'

There was something about the selectivity, the fatal sense of privilege already seen in every gesture and thought of the Lovescombe family, which won me over – as, doubtless, it had won so many before me. Frightened – of the power of the Azeby myth, of a society, hardly known it seemed by the world at large, which could still maintain these great houses much as they had been before the 'lost' generation went to purge in blood the excesses of beauty and brute expropriation – I was all the same intrigued to be, if only temporarily, 'one of them'. I went with Amy under a wooden gateway, hacked like a king's house in pre-history, tempered by wind and rain, stained with lichen, hung over with creeper so that a curtain must be pushed aside to leave the atrium and go further in. Above us, the treehouse became more clearly visible. I was awestruck at the enduringness, the solidity of this fantasy of permanent immaturity. Tiles on the gabled roof were lichen-dyed too, but in good repair. Windows of coloured glass, unbroken, wood-dusty but bright, glittered in the rays of the sun. The whole structure was hung between a collection of trees that would by themselves have constituted the masts of a fair-sized galleon. And beyond where Amy and I now stood was the facsimile of a medieval village. This was built round a 'green', so green indeed it looked as if no one had ever walked on it; a green with a white gleam of mushrooms. Round the green were 'ancient' buildings: 'oast house', 'granary', dovecote battered grey with the long winters since it was last filled with doves; then a long building that, for one moment of unintentional irreverence I took to be a form of poorhouse: picturesque, communal, a door half leaning on its hinges and the outline of furniture stored inside, where once there had been derelicts, vagrants, claimants of grazing rights and turf, all long gone but for the equally picturesque dialect which Lady

Azeby had loved to render in her after-dinner speeches in the white drawing-room at Lovegrove. But I was wrong in this. 'The old Racquet Court,' Amy said, seeing me stare. 'People played tennis. And look – that's where they kept the ice.' She pointed to a hump – not unlike the barrows on the downs and in the woods where we had come; this one had an iron grille door, though, and again there was a glimpse, this time of steps going down, murky with mulched leaves. I thought of the steps going down under the earth and meeting the chalk water of the tributaries of the River Love as they flowed there; and then of the long trek by the pantry-man in his white apron to an underground house of ice. Amy skirted the green, under trees so huge it was impossible to think of them felled or ageing, even: oaks, and magnificent beeches that arched to the sky and grew at their feet in winter aisles of snowdrops and yellow aconite. Box hedges long unclipped screened Amy from me suddenly, and I had to run to catch up, scourged by branches that were strong-smelling, leaf-dust gold.

I should have realized Amy wanted to lose me in this way – to make the shock of the discovery greater for me perhaps: that shock of sudden understanding. For of course, the village, the green, the timber house with gabled roofs high in the trees were the playthings of a giant, a gigantic infant: the real house had its back to us here. Behind the high, pungent hedge was the first hint of more flagstones and then the widening out into a skirt of cobblestones; three walls enclosed a courtyard while the fourth, cut off from the main house, was a stable block, startling with red creeper, decrepit in door and hinge, facing the back of the old house with its windows under cataracts of age and dust. No sign of Amy, though. A yew almost as tall as the great trees on the pretended 'green' blocked the passageway between courtyard and the front of the house, with its circle of grass by the door, and a raised rose garden up a flight of steps. The stones went down to yellow slips, wafer stones that were harder underfoot, and led past the great yew, a rustle of climbing white roses caught in its sombre branches, on to a sandy circle (not gravel, as I had imagined, and a feeling unpleasantly reminiscent of childhood fear, of sandy lanes, a fox at the end and a waiting victim). The far side of the sand surround led to the flight of steps, some chipped at the sides, that climbed to the raised garden. An air of absolute exhaustion emanated from it, an air of dog-days, of roses waiting for the nip in the bud. More yews ringed a stone bench, a round stone table, and a hammock stretched between two trunks of flaking bark. I reached the top of the steps, knowing I wouldn't find Amy there; seeing instead the reclining figure of a man in a robe such as I had seen only in childhood picture-books of Lawrence of Arabia ('not my cup of tea', Aunt Babs had said, as if these representations of the desert, the flowing robes and the bright sky beyond were in some way repugnant to her).

The figure in the hammock must have heard my steps for it moved slightly, portly under a white garment none too clean. The face, I saw, was made up: powder, a bright white with a tinge of green – 'an arsenic Burne-Jones', as Walter Neet was to pronounce later on 'Uncle Si', as this indeed turned out to be, when he heard of my and Amy's visit to the House in the Woods. Vermilion lips made up the rest, eyes languorous under lids as innocent a blue as those Arabian skies so hated by Aunt Babs. He must have been at least fifty-five. A straggle of blond, greying chest-hair poked out from the frogged opening of the djellaba (as, again, I was informed later this clothing was called).

Amy was staring out at us from a first-floor window of the house. I saw her only because I stepped away from the hammock and its disturbing Oriental burden to the far side of one of the yews supporting it. I thought I had never seen such a gulf as lay between me and safety – if Amy could be said to represent safety – but, at the same time, I felt that to descend the chipped steps, cross the sand circle in front of the house, push open the thick wooden door and call for her to come down might invite some sudden – and terrifying – movement. So I stood by the round beds of yellow roses, waiting, I thought, in vain, for Amy wore her mischievous look, a look no doubt from her childhood at Lovegrove, and suggesting she might leave me in my rose-scented bazaar while she slipped home another way, probably to greet Candida.

As it happened, the decision was taken out of my hands. The thick oak door swung open, a burst of voices came out across the mound of grass encircled by reddish sand, and at the same time Amy's head vanished from the window and the supine figure behind me stirred – having decided, perhaps, that I was a hallucination, a not very important one at that, but that voices were infinitely more threatening.

Certainly the voices carried an intimidating ring. I came down from the raised garden with a sense of falling from some heavenly place, of being expelled from a bower which, like the treehouse, was built in an age of children dressed as soldiers or sailors or in farmers' smocks: all representations of that 'innocence' attributed to the lower classes of Edwardian fancy (what would Lady Azeby have made of her son's caftan, I later wondered: it was hardly possible to tame the bedouin in their tents). I reached almost to the bottom when a tone of loud laughter emanating from the hall froze me yet again in my pose. I had a ridiculous sensation of being a part of 'Grandmother's footsteps', where to turn and glimpse a moving figure at the rear is to send them back to base; and a stronger feeling

of being about to receive a blow in the back from the
enraged owner of this secret house. To step forward was
to come face to face with that raucous, familiar laugh. Again
the decision was taken from me, the door pulling even
further open and three people stepping out, nameless apart
from the laughter, on to the sand.

Carmen – for she it was whose voice had taken me back
to the last days at school – looked if anything wilder than
before. A kind of grim determination appeared to possess
her as she turned to look up at the façade of the house –
provoking, in me at least, a sense that the house flinched
back at the sight of her. Argumentativeness and ill-temper
had also, it was clear, accompanied Carmen on her holiday,
for the man in the party (its other member was a startling-
looking girl with white-yellow hair below the waist) was
speaking in a quiet and 'humouring' voice, pointing out,
as if to a child, the features of the building, while Carmen
growled back at him or alternatively exploded in one of her
monumental bellows of mirth. I took the opportunity to
glance behind me – made bolder perhaps by the knowledge
of possessing the name and details of this unwelcome visitor; and saw that the robed figure had indeed been stopped
in his tracks by the influx. He seemed to be peering down
with some anxiety at the man in the group, the women very
likely being as awful to him as a pair of young bulls met in
a country lane; the man, however, was slow to look up or
afford assistance, explanations even of why or how they
had come.

'I'm really sorry, Uncle Si!' Amy burst out the front door.
Carmen's laugh, puzzled at first, gained in strength when
she saw me – and then, on seeing Amy, redoubled. 'You
never told me we'd see Amy here,' she half-shouted at the
man, who had turned away with an expression – or so it
seemed from my stance in the amphitheatre – of sallow

loathing and disgust. 'Hey, Jenny, I had no idea you were going to be here.'

The man's arm was now pulled; and still with a look of one who is both tormented by inner visions and at the same time in the presence of something utterly repugnant, he turned to Amy and said his name was Bernard Ehrlich. 'We are going to Lovegrove for lunch,' was the ensuing statement; this said, a silence still echoing with the disturbance of Carmen's laughter fell once more on the round of grass that marked the front drive's swoop to main road or to stables and courtyard. A hush followed, breathed out by the yews and the giant beeches of Lady Azeby's monumental treehouse. 'Now we're here,' Ehrlich said, half-bowing in the direction of 'Uncle Si', to whom he had not yet been introduced, 'it would be most interesting to see round the house.'

Contrary to all expectations, this request lightened the air at once. 'Uncle Si' came down the steps past me with a skipping run and, reaching the circle of grass, held out a hand; a hand which – bedecked as it was with bright stones and a gush of bracelets that slid from wrist to half-cover the palm – could then be seen, by virtue of an unexpected side opening in the djellaba, to be attached to an arm of extraordinary whiteness. We all stared at this arm – and at the bright, sickly arrangement of gems and sparkle at the end of it – for some time before conversation broke out again. Certainly Carmen, Bernard Ehrlich and the mermaid-like girl were transfixed by the appearance of 'Uncle Si', and only Amy (who was well used to it, I had to suppose, although she had never, like so many other aspects of her life at Lovegrove, spoken of him to me) seeming unaffected by it – even effortlessly interpreting the babble of words which now escaped from 'Uncle Si's' lips in the same bright, sliding cluster as the jewels at his wrist.

'Uncle Si says he wasn't expecting you and he'd like to go and put his Spanish combs in,' Amy said, after some of this un-transcribable patter had gone on. 'He says to go inside, then to go out the far side onto Sunset Boulevard.'

There was no doubt that, in our different ways, we were all equally excited by this. The mermaid, giving her name suddenly to Amy as 'Sonia Fount', seemed both to belong entirely to the ambience of this buried treasure of the sensibilities of the twenties and thirties, a sort of Hollywood forty fathoms down under the trees (for this was where, in his own level of childhood, it soon became clear 'Uncle Si' had 'stuck'), and to show her own awakening to the possibilities that lay ahead, these being acutely glimpsed by 'Uncle Si' himself, who murmured as he went past at a strange run of his own devising, that she was as lovely as a Lorelei, Jean Harlow-fair. Bernard Ehrlich, whom I could now study with a little more attention, succeeded in intimating that he had known all along what to expect in the home of the second son of the great Lady Azeby, but went so far as to show a glimmer of interest in the proceedings, his reptilian features then sinking into repose again immediately, to remind anyone interested that nothing moved or indeed could ever move such long-quenched appetites. I wondered what it was like to 'sit' for him, calling to mind Aunt Babs' refusal to allow various visitors to talk of Bernard Ehrlich's 'habits' in my presence; and with a sudden flash realized that Carmen, by her rude, proprietorial and generally jeering stance, must be one of his 'sitters', an intuition borne out later that afternoon when, at long last and at the request of Bernard Ehrlich, we were taken by Lord Lovescombe into the room of 'Modern Art' where Miss Carston hoped her brother would one day hang, and saw, it being particularly hard to avert the eyes from either subject or original (for she was on the tour with us) a carcass suspended between two blue ropes, a head affixed as an afterthought, the point of focus being a vulva the size of an average pub-sign and emerging, as if caught by the painter in the midst of a gruesome disembowelling ceremony, straight out of the canvas and, so to speak, on to our laps: all this, going by the expression of rage on the face at least, belonging to Carmen.

As I say, I had no idea of this when we all trooped into the hall of 'Uncle Si's' house and made our way, as directed, to windows open at the back of the large, square hall; but it's possible that a sense of Carmen's sexuality, of her having 'done it' at long last in reality, after all the boasting and fantasies of our schooldays at St Peter's, pervaded me as I toured this shrine to the sex-drug of Hollywood, the framed faces of Betty Grable, Bette Davis, Marlene, that gave off, like strong-smelling flowers at a funeral, a waft of poison-scented air. Nothing could have been further, as I was to learn after lunch that day, from the stark social realism, or (later) expressionism of Ehrlich's style. Carmen's dismembered trunk, head with rolling eyes on the point of decapitation, her proffered 'private parts' (as my Aunt Babs would have referred to this most public of advertisements) were, it seemed, the property of another race to these golden goddesses.

While I pondered the details of Carmen's new life, 'Uncle Si' had darted downstairs again, this time with hair held up by the promised Spanish combs, holding in outstretched hands a single madonna lily, and suggesting a wine – some kind of golden wine, if I remember – intimating at least by his mellifluous tones and semi-fantastic utterances that we were to take nectar with him – all in this house of Lady Azeby's spiritual dreams which had been turned into a cross between Shangri-La and the local Odeon. Carmen accepted the invitation with zeal: 'Uncle Si', however, showed his preference for the pale girl, a probable reject of Ehrlich's, who stood beside him in the polar-bear and Thai-silk-strewn hall with a sad, used-up expression, looking (or so I thought suddenly in my attempt to 'see' Ehrlich, the first 'real' painter I had met, a professional as dedicated to his art as Aunt Babs' Camden Town friends were amateurs) like a paintbrush in a glass of water, this impression only reinforced by the straggle of pale hair at her neck and thin, brown-stained legs. 'Uncle Si' had seen possibilities in the girl, though, and on being told that she was Sonia Fount burst into a ripple of laughter which, accompanied as it now was by a sip from one of the goblets brought in by an aged retainer, made me move over to Carmen; she, strangely enough, being the one who seemed the more 'ordinary' of the two girls. (I thought Amy affected then, I must confess, by the heritage of Lovegrove, the family passing down over the generations its side-angle view of life, a view obscured by wealth and privilege, as if the high bridge of the aquiline Azeby nose acted as a sort of flying buttress from which it was impossible to see anything but oneself.)

I half expected, I admit, to step out on the terrace – which we were now being encouraged to do – and find the whole place had magically risen to the tree-platform of the Azeby children's youth. So, on coming nearer to the long windows to the terrace, I was glad to see the ground, even if it was terracotta rather than terra firma, nevertheless conjoined at some way off by a lawn and clumps of bushes. Carmen took my arm, her expression now changed to one of avid excitement: 'Well, Jenny.' As we went, we looked sideways into rooms originally 'done' in the taste of Lady Azeby: the Morris chrysanthemums now swagged over with red damask, gold tassels, confectioners' cornices, as if a succession of the Pollocks toy theatres of childhood had been set up, to while away long hours of boredom with matinées, intervals, evening dress. 'There's some swag here all right.' I glanced with anxiety at Carmen as she said this. Amy was just behind us with 'Uncle Si' and the silent, 'March-pale' (for this was his epithet for her) Sonia Fount. We all paused, as if in some procession at the Court of the Sun King, to allow 'Uncle Si' to pick a vine leaf at the entrance to the tiled terrace known as Sunset Boulevard. This, slid with great dexterity on to another smaller leaf and bound with the filaments of a fig stem, was presented to the young heiress – for so she proved to be – as a ring to be placed upon her finger. 'All the colours of the rainbow in the drop of water on this leaf,' said 'Uncle Si', comprehensibly at least, but still in tones of great urgency and to the company in general; while Ehrlich, eyes half-closed as if in agony at the thought of the contemplation of the wonders of the natural world, strolled out into the artificial sunset and took up an odd, half-crouched position by a wicker chair, which, long left out in the rain, was grey and broken, an incongruous reminder of the Azeby past in a setting of silver and gold palms, marble basins of mosaic-flecked water alive with the dapple of fish, and pillars suggesting the imminent arrival of Pearl and Dean.

I thought of this odd combination, seeing suddenly that what had caused alarm in me was the absolute refusal here to distinguish between the real and the imagined world; and, as if transported myself to this Tantric state by the psychic waves of 'Uncle Si', I too began to see the strangeness of the assumptions of the 'real' world, whether those of 'money-men' such as Lord Lovescombe or 'nice people' like my Aunt Babs. There seemed, in short, to be no way of telling the fake from the real, the literal from the figurative in 'Uncle Si's' house: this meant, too, an absence of judgement of what was right and wrong, the whole place resembling somehow the mind and preoccupations of a child before the age in which a moral sense sets in. I had an uneasy feeling, too, that Carmen, in representing for me the real world – for I had little choice, in my need to get away from the Azeby inheritance, and, of the rest, Sonia Fount was too ethereal to provide support and Ehrlich too much like the trolls of my early Red, Yellow and Green Fairybooks – that Carmen was also influenced by this lack of concern for moral propriety; and that others, as she was shortly to explain, had 'gone before' was of no consequence to her at all. 'Bernard says they come down and pull notes out of their pockets,' Carmen said, describing further the 'dealers' who she said found their way to 'Uncle Si'. I imagined them as truffle-hounds, scenting the rich pickings of the strange old duffer who lived in a fairy ring in the middle of the woods, knocking on the back door and, once admitted by the white-gloved, shaking-fingered retainer, being led proudly to the treasures Lady Azeby had left her eccentric heir. The rest was almost too painful to contemplate. 'Lord Lovescombe's always worrying about it, so they say,' Carmen went on recklessly, for we were well within earshot of the party, having pulled back from Sunset Boulevard into a sort of ante-room which, from the relics of blue and white – a vase here, a low chair there, in the upholstery created by William Morris and his Utopians – had probably been a 'boudoir' of Lady Azeby's. We stood by a squat window looking out on the end of the terrace, where were a battered dovecote and the last stretch of dyed-pink sand. Through the artificial palms fringing the terrace I could see water. A feeling of doubt – not unexpectedly, in such a place – took hold of me. The water was green and foamed slightly, as if stirred by some unseen minion of 'Uncle Si's'. Hollywood-Roman-orgy scenes suggested themselves, or a bubble-bath for a great star at least, an outsize cube of bath salts having been dropped in to stimulate motion. At the same time, doubt pushed itself more powerfully to the front of my mind. What if this was the weir, of which Amy and Lord Lovescombe had spoken, at which indeed they had agreed to meet 'before lunch', although any concept of ordinary time at 'Uncle Si's' had long ago disappeared. Had we followed the river in our walk through the wood? Was our return to take place along the banks of this secret tributary of the Avon, its meandering, sylvan path jealously guarded by the Lovescombe family?

By now Carmen had moved ahead, leaving the anteroom and passing into a wide room, bay-windowed, from which she could not be seen from the terrace or the main hall. Not for the first time, I wondered how she came to be here. Was it really the case that Bernard Ehrlich, with whom she had clearly 'formed a strong attachment', as the more formidable spinsters of Aunt Babs' circle liked to describe such things, had accepted an invitation to Lovegrove without telling Carmen where they were expected to lunch? I came to the conclusion that this was highly probable. A man like Ehrlich, moving around the country with a woman or two in tow, would hardly spare the time to explain the itinerary to them: the dazed expression of Sonia Fount, at least, showing that geography was of little concern to her: that she lived, as the models and mistresses of Ehrlich were said to do, entirely within the confines of his regard, cruelty or indifference. It wasn't hard to see that Carmen, who had the appearance of having reacted to Ehrlich in quite a different way from Sonia Fount, with a kind of snarling, wounded pride I had sometimes seen in her when she was in 'trouble' at school, was the more likely of the two to break free. It was this, perhaps, that made me follow her with some apprehension into the wide, deep-set room where stood a round table, used presumably in the early days for eating but littered now with shells, pebbles and plates spilling over with semi-precious stones. Carmen was standing by the table. I went up to her – at slightly too great a speed, it seemed, for she jumped back and crashed into me, an object flying from her hand as she went and landing, unbroken, on the floor by my feet.

'Carmen!' I stood helpless over the object – a white china dove – and knew if I stooped to retrieve it I'd be found there with booty in my hand. 'For God's sake, Carmen, put that back!'

Carmen, who was carrying a large black bag, paid no attention to this. She picked up the dove (which, from my visits to the V & A with Aunt Babs, I could identify as a 'Chelsea dove' and probably one of a pair) and slipped it nonchalantly into the bag. I stared at Carmen, aware at the same time of the party of people coming in from the terrace; of the fact that I must have been carrying my goblet with me (and drinking the dizzying contents as I went) and had put it down on the casual arrangement of stones and shells that littered the central table so that it stood at an angle, the rose-crystal glass seeming to be a part of 'Uncle Si's' arrangement; and of Amy's voice, discontented, as so often on the afternoons in the long summer term, which reminded me again of my impending isolation on the arrival of Candida. For a moment, I have to confess, I thought of denouncing Carmen's theft of the dove, thus calling attention to myself (and occasioning gratitude, no doubt, from Amy at averting the 'trouble' which would inevitably ensue when its disappearance was noticed) but, seeing Carmen's eye sternly fixed on me, some failure of courage stopped me from doing so. I had no thought then of right or wrong: 'Uncle Si's' house, as I have tried to describe, precluded, perhaps by the very unusual way in which objects of both virtue, necessity and semi-luxury were arranged there in a haphazard way, any sense of the permanence or dignity of ownership. This in itself lent the dove, very possibly, some of the almost mystical beauty I saw in it.

'Uncle Si' came into the room followed by Bernard Ehrlich and Sonia Fount, from whom Ehrlich (in his desire, probably, not to be seen as part of a couple with either of the girls) was keeping as far as possible. I was reminded of the illustrations in an Arthur Crane book of Beauty and the Beast, kept by my parents until they went abroad and then returned to Aunt Babs, those books being considered very valuable in the days when, the glories of Victorian and Edwardian illustration being long over, children of my generation were expected to enjoy a diet of Enid Blyton. In the book I remembered, the beast, head down, made for a bush of white roses where Beauty was concealed; and although Sonia Fount could hardly be said to be beautiful – in the way Crane or Dulac, say, would have portrayed such a quality – her extreme pallor, combined with the fact that 'Uncle Si' had placed a spray of roses in her hand, to accompany the madonna lily mysteriously brought down earlier, made her entrance bridal – and was also the reason, possibly, for Ehrlich's convincing impersonation of Jekyll on the way to becoming Hyde. Amy brought up the rear of this unconvincing couple. I could see at once from her face, as I had heard from her voice on the terrace, that she was bored, and impatient to get away. 'Uncle Si' also showed signs of wear and tear, as if these fleeting dreams in his afternoon rest in the hammock must fly off soon, leaving him time for the empty, memoryless sleep of a child.

'Jenny!' Amy said. 'We'd better go.' And, Carmen stepping forward at this and swinging the bag with a casualness that made my heart sink, she added quickly: 'And you, Carmen. Come on.'

'We'll go back through the wood,' Bernard Ehrlich now said, indicating (surprisingly in the circumstances) Sonia Fount.

Farewells were made, these being brief as 'Uncle Si's' hours ran to a nursery timetable, the sweet wine when served at all being a liqueur after his meal; his bedtime coming 'when the daisies close their eyes and the bluebells droop their heads', Amy said, laughing (but as if these sayings of 'Uncle Si' were repeated often as a joke among the Lovescombes and their guests, refreshing, perhaps, the exhausted mind of Jim Tremlett after too long a perusal of *The Waste Land*). Now we headed out across Sunset Boulevard – as I had seen, the river lay at the bottom of the garden and the weir, darker now as rain threatened, surged beyond – 'Uncle Si' having sent his most effusive waves to Ehrlich and Sonia Fount as they crossed the polar-bear skins in the main hall and set off down the drive.

CHAPTER ELEVEN

We walked a while in silence, Amy leading and Carmen behind her, like figures on a Greek vase, the second maiden in this case bearing a bucket bag, newly in fashion at that time, which would surely fall and shatter its priceless contents on the ground. I decided to keep my eyes averted from this almost certain disaster for as long as possible: there was the weir to contemplate as we grew closer, over the short meadow grass at the end of 'Uncle Si's' garden, and there was a sky as violently technicolour as 'Uncle Si' himself could possibly hope for, the crude blues and purples of a previously fine day massaged by long black clouds. I thought of the English predilection for weather, and (I confess with another pang of homesickness) of Aunt Babs in her pollen-blown garden looking up at the sky over Paddington, musing on the trip to the West Country she was always about to take, laughing again over a reputed remark by the king, who had died only last year, King George VI, to the artist John Piper, on visiting an exhibition of his watercolours, that he 'must have had very bad weather'.

This memory unfortunately returning me to Lord Lovescombe's collection of modern art, and hence to the white Chelsea dove in Carmen's bag, I tried to think of everything but the odd and dangerous situation I found myself in (for I felt sure I would be blamed for the theft of the dove and that I would be sent back to Aunt Babs a branded criminal) and concentrated now on the figure that came to us along the path by the weir – or rather, two figures. I could tell from Amy abruptly stopping that the entwined form these two figures made was unacceptable to her in the extreme. That it was Lord Lovescombe and Jasmine Tremlett I felt sure: that Amy's father should be so brazen as to walk like this with (a term of Aunt Babs' military acquaintance again) his 'paramour' seemed, quite simply, incredible. In my last unavailing effort to distance myself from the scene, I bent down and stared at the rushing water of the weir, the pool beyond and the Love as it joined the River Avon. This I saw for the first time in its broad sweep west of Salisbury before it entered the domain of Lovegrove and went off south again, feeding on its way the tributaries and 'cuts' of the floating world of the Lovescombe estate and fortune. On the far bank, beyond the weir and a rickety-looking wooden humpback bridge, were the water-meadows I had seen from my bedroom window in the dawn; a herd of cows, sitting (this was a sign, Amy said, that rain was coming on) now under the willows; others munched on buttercups in grassy ditches not more than a couple of feet deep, so that they looked half-cut off at the knee, like a child's farmyard picture-book torn in two. I thought of the early morning, and Ludo, and the invisible girl, her bare toes curled up over the armrest of the nursery sofa, her slipper kicked off, and knew I was led back always to one thing, invisible most of the time as the girl had been, yet pressing on me more and more: the incessant question of sexuality, of love for Amy and the (misplaced, as even I could see) love for Ludo that was growing in me: the need for love and the shrinking from it; all this brought to mind yet again, no doubt, by the sight of the entwined figures, who were coming closer to us now along a grass path that seemed to have been mown to accommodate them, with trees almost comically operatic framing their approach. 'Let's cut through the wood,' Amy said. 'Jenny, there's a bit of garden I want you – to see.'

'I dunno.' Carmen was presumably under the impression she had been invited too to see this 'bit' of garden (I was to dream, for many years, of the patchwork of different gardens at Lovegrove, the green of the water-garden, the massed roses along the stone walls of the vegetable garden above the house and, beyond this, through an entrance of arched yews, a garden higher than 'Uncle Si's' raised garden where I had found him slung in his hammock between the masts of his afternoon ship – a woodland garden where 'things from the north' as Amy was vaguely to put it, grew: a place where I could think of Ludo as he walked the moors at Castle Azeby). Carmen said: 'I think it's nicer down here by the river, Amy.'

Aware sometimes at school of an underlying arrogance and impatience in Amy, I was also often surprised by a tolerance – and by a quality which, I felt with some guilt, would never be mine because of some inherent pettiness in my nature: a generosity, a desire that people shouldn't feel left out. It was perhaps because this quality was so strong in Amy that her occasional tactlessness, or her inability to understand the feelings of others, as with the casual breaking of the news of Candida's imminent arrival, was so devastating. There was no doubt that Amy had greeted Carmen's unexpected presence at 'Uncle Si's' with some reserve. Thinking, very likely, that an expulsion from school followed by a long summer break might end any relationship she and Carmen had had (and there had been one: to return to Amy's faults, she found it too easy to forget earlier feelings – the 'naughty side', as when she and

147

Carmen had done the impersonation of Lady Pickering, had sparked off a fairly strong sense of complicity and shared fun), Amy had undoubtedly been cool at seeing Carmen again. Putting this down to the unreal atmosphere at 'Uncle Si's', I half expected a burst of chatter and interested questions as soon as we got away from Sunset Boulevard and on to the comparative ordinariness of the river bank. Amy had gone on in silence, however, and Carmen, bearer of the dove, had gone unheard (or at least heard only by me) as she spoke of recent adventures, these including the 'gambling man' to whose flat she claimed to have been taken and sold to a Greek millionaire, redeeming herself only by winning a huge pile at the tables and buying herself free; and excluding, I noted, her relationship with Bernard Ehrlich, possibly the only thing that had really happened to her. I speculated on my own feelings of superiority over Carmen, and then on their unsuitability, given my own increasing fantasies on the subject of Amy's brother, the difference, I concluded, being that I kept these to myself and made no pretence, even to myself, that I had any chance of converting my dream into reality. Amy, still walking in ignorance of the stolen goods being carried behind her, now turned to Carmen with that sweetness of which I felt so protective that I had to wonder, sometimes, if I weren't simply jealous of Amy being kind to anyone other than me. 'Oh, do come, Carmen. It's really fun seeing you again – here.'

This was said with some effort, an effort which went unnoticed by Carmen who, stopping suddenly once more behind Amy, crashed the bag into the back of her legs. I stared out at the river again, my heart beating so that the steps of the approaching entwined couple were muffled by the sounds of my own agitation. I wouldn't be asking her on a walk, myself, I thought with increased irritation, feeling tempted again to blurt out the contents of the bag which, tied with something that looked like an old boot-lace, now dangled just a foot from the path as Carmen, with almost unbelievable insouciance, bent down and untied the lace, searching in the interior for something or other. For a moment I thought she might confess, and in the face of Amy's kindness and friendliness hand the dove back; then, as it became apparent that this was not the case, I tried to shoot Amy a warning glance which, like most warning glances, was first ignored and then misinterpreted, Amy even rewarding me for my efforts with a scowl. 'Must have a fag,' Carmen said, finally extricating a crushed packet of Weights from the 'bucket'. 'Anyone got a match?'

It would be difficult to say which caused the most embar-rassment at this point: Carmen's blatant breaking of 'the rules' (which, unspoken for the reason that to accept the crime's existence, would, like lesbianism in the reign of Queen Victoria, be partly to condone it: for smoking, never referred to at St Peter's, would certainly have resulted in expulsion; while at Lovegrove, in all probability, total iso-lation in some untenanted part of the house would ensue, for Lady Lovescombe, madonna-white in all her aspects, frowned on 'the weed' except when inhaled by those with a distinctly literary or artistic character); or, to return to the question of maximum embarrassment for Amy at that moment, the proximity of the entwined couple on the river path. Even I, short-sighted from an early age, was able to recognize an outline that was in no way reminiscent of Jasmine Tremlett's, while the male, still loping, half-hugging his companion, bore no resemblance whatsoever to Lord Lovescombe. Amy, eyes distracted from the cigarette which was now cocked between Carmen's fingers, stiff-ened and stood back a couple of paces, coming dangerously near as she did so to stepping into the river. Her action 'put up' a coot, which skimmed the water diagonally and then went fast upstream, sensing, perhaps, an explosive combination of temperaments on the river bank or, given the sudden flame which spurted in the hand of the approaching man, remembering the scene of carnage that took place on evening duck-shoots by the river, when a spray of bright beads of fire went up against a darkening sky. 'Thanks,' Carmen said, drawing in smoke, speaking again through a thin blue plume, 'So how's things, Candida?'

There was little doubt that the owner of the chunky American lighter (of a make never before seen in England, as was the case with most desirable and unobtainable things at that period, American) was the man of whom both Amy and Candida had spoken the previous summer when, after a holiday spent in the north – at Castle Azeby, I knew – they had 'fallen in love' with Mick Scupper, invited to value the pictures and library in the Lovescombes' northern estate, for tax and inheritance purposes. Scupper, whose pencilled features, in various forms, had appeared the following term in both Amy and Candida's 'rough' books, superimposed on algebra practice or French vocabulary, was also the owner, as I recalled being breathlessly informed by Candida, of a long American car, a Thunderbird it was called; and for the first time, remembering the fantasies which Carmen constructed for herself and knowing also their occasional foundation in truth, I wondered if the 'gigantic great American car' which Carmen boasted waited for her sometimes at the corner of Hammersmith Broadway wasn't in fact Scupper's.

Whether or not this was the case, Amy certainly looked put out by the bounding zeal of Scupper, who was, indeed, much as the doodles of early infatuation in the 'rough' books had shown him: tall and good-looking in a way that illustrators of journals for women of the time liked to represent, a 'quiff' of hair hanging over one side of a lean and almost triangular face; while Candida, slightly pink from the exertion of the forced run along the river bank, looked as put out as Amy at being first seen in this unacceptable pose. 'Hello, Jenny.' Candida had clearly decided that to address Amy might be a wrong move, might even result in a backward move on Amy's part, ending in an ignominious fall in the river. It was clear, too, from Candida's mime of coincidental meetings – to Scupper she held out her hands as if in amazement at having 'bumped into' him further down the river bank; to Amy and me she held out her arms with a kind of shy stiffness, as if to show her good luck at coming across us here, of all places, and to Carmen she quite simply turned a shoulder, showing that she had not expected her here, and therefore she was not here – that Candida was still as crude an actress as when, putting in for the part with which Amy had effortlessly charmed the school, she had caused the drama teacher to burst out laughing. It wasn't that she was 'transparent' as is sometimes said of the guileless, more that her different reactions to different echelons of people – as Candida must have perceived the human race – conflicted with each other painfully if she was in the company of more than one person at a time. Hence we stood on the river bank while these attitudes, all with a jerkiness of movement suggesting a mechanical doll, were played out; and it was Carmen, not included in the succession of charades, who insisted on getting an answer to her enquiry on the subject of Candida's health. 'How're things?' Carmen repeated.

Mick Scupper clearly noted the air of strain between Amy and Candida, saw too, with an experienced flicker of the eye, the wild improbabilities already under construction in the mind of Carmen. He assured us all of his recent arrival at Lovegrove: 'I wasn't sure where I'd find you. Made over a hundred on the way down, did it in under two hours and then zap! the house is completely deserted when I get there!' – all said, I couldn't help noticing, as if he were addressing an impatient board meeting at the very least; at the worst, a jury. Candida's 'My train was exactly on time at Salisbury. It was so sweet to be met by Vine,' was, in the circumstances, an even more unnecessary statement. Both of these justifications, I came to the conclusion, constituted an effort to show they had met quite accidentally in the garden and had run along the river bank or, rather, Scupper had pulled Candida along with him in the eager, 'rough' way young men then affected.

Amy said it was time we were getting back. The absence of her father, whom we had been going to meet at the weir, had made her forget the time, 'But I expect he couldn't be bothered to wait, and he can't have known we'd go to Uncle Si's.' This was said with a sweet smile in Candida's direction, the sweetness deceiving me at first, until, as Candida's expression registered, I remembered Amy's streak of cruelty as well as the battery of weapons at her disposal, Candida having doubtless been told many times of the wonders and treasures of 'Uncle Si's' and now finding herself arrived too late at Lovegrove to see them. Worst of all, I had got there first. Amy now turned to me and, as if to punish Candida further for her mode of entry on the scene, said she and I would go back, as she'd earlier said we would, by the 'bit of garden' she wanted me to see. So saying, she set out, crossing one of the small planks that were half-hidden by rushes and flag iris, to the less boggy ground beyond. I followed; Candida, Scupper and, bringing up the rear, Carmen turned and made their way back along the towpath to the house.

CHAPTER TWELVE

It was hard to know whether Amy would appreciate any questions about Mick Scupper. The time of the recklessly filled 'rough' book had been comparatively brief; and while it was clear that 'something happened' in the summer holidays at the Lovescombes' northern outpost, it was generally assumed to have been the kind of thing liable to 'happen' to a girl of fourteen – in those days, at any rate – that is to say, nothing. A glance had probably been exchanged; addresses probably not; Amy's air of concealed excitement, accompanied by sketches which would have won no prizes with Miss Carston, wore off after a week or two, while Candida had no comment to make at all. I realized, on that walk along the river bank, that I had been wrong: that Amy's flippant, sometimes distant behaviour in the past year could all have been a mask to hide a passion made all the more powerful by an enforced separation from the loved one. Certainly Candida's arrival, which I had foreseen as a signal of my own coming loneliness at Lovegrove, could now be regarded in a very different light, Amy's obvious jealousy of her self-appointed best friend sending her very likely in my direction and away from Candida – a possibility which, though causing suffering to Amy, I could only welcome. I wondered how long Scupper was planning to stay at Lovegrove; how long, indeed, he had stayed at Castle Azeby the previous summer, when the fatal seeds had clearly been sown. Amy took some of the vagueness from my thoughts by beginning to speak – at this point we had left the others some way behind and were crossing the carpet of beech leaves again, climbing now away from the river and up a part of the wood only skirted before. I could feel my breath come in uneven gasps, and Amy's speech was punctuated by short pants for breath, lending a spurious air of melodrama to her account of the summer with Candida and Mick Scupper.

'We all went to the Mare's Tail.' Amy stopped and I did the same. We were almost at the top of the bank. The trees here were even more surreal than those we had walked under on the way to 'Uncle Si's', reminiscent of the then newly imported Walt Disney films of which Aunt Babs so much disapproved. 'The Mare's Tail is the longest waterfall in England,' Amy went on. 'It's just on the borders of Scotland, where we live.' (I have to admit I was confused at this, imagining that Amy would see herself as 'living' in London and possibly also at Lovegrove, but doing little more than 'going to' the house in the north.) 'We all went – me, and Candida and the Tremletts, who were staying, and Mick.'

For a moment I was so distracted by the idea of the Tremletts in Border Country – a picture of Jasmine running naked in the heather came to mind, then another of Jasmine dodging behind a cairn to avoid detection – that I was unable to focus on the mention of 'Mick'. When I did I saw that, despite the physiological reasons for Amy's gasping delivery, she seemed to be in a highly emotional state. The trip to the Mare's Tail was clearly a trip that would never be forgotten, the first signpost to the ending of childhood, perhaps, in a suitably romantic setting, the plume of great water falling in the craggy hills serving as any amount of symbols for those interested in employing them. I asked Amy what had happened at the Mare's Tail; feeling, as I did so, a by now familiar pang at the thought of Ludo standing beside the long streak of water or, blond hair windswept and eyes piercing the apparently uninhabited moors, raising a gun to bring down a hare got up suddenly among the grey slate stones. I thought of absence: in the case of Amy, an absence of a year which must have caused her great agitation, particularly as the time of Scupper's scheduled visit to value the art treasures of the Lovescombes drew near; and of the dreams that grow in absence, as mine of Ludo were doing: dreams as large, frightening and seemingly real as the shadows thrown by the giant beeches where we stood. Then we began to climb again — and stopped once more to catch breath, the way to the top of the cliff a painful scramble in the last vertiginous stretch. A plateau of short, scrubby grass opened out in front of us. I thought of the absence, too, in Amy's life, of Lady Lovescombe, remote in another sense as my own mother in the war had been to me, in her sojourns at one house or another, or on her buying trips abroad to add to the Lovescombe collection of modern art, while Amy stayed with a nanny (this she had told me: her memory of childhood would always be the bars of a night-nursery window, wherever this might be, an archetypically Victorian image). Too inchoate to be described as thoughts, my feelings encompassed some of the great mistakes which lay ahead for both of us: the compelling need to fill that absence with love and security, and the premonition that such things proved only too often chimeras, insubstantial as the play of light and shade that gave the trees around us an air of cartwheeling: a circus of trees, dancing round us in a ring, joining hands in an illusion of love and happiness. The reality, I could

155

sense, was the grim, cold truth of circumstance, effort, work. But for that moment I felt the longing in Amy, the need for fulfilment, and I felt it too, my imagination fixed on the green slopes and rocky chasms of the country round Castle Azeby.

'So what happened there?' I asked.

'Where? Oh, you mean the Mare's Tail.' Just as my thoughts had fixed themselves up there, so must Amy's have strayed off somewhere else. She laughed. 'Nothing really happened. It was just – Daddy . . .' She paused, looking out from the plateau at downs in a chalky smudge going off into a sky the same pale indeterminate wash. I wondered why we had come as far from Lovegrove as this, in order to return there in time for lunch: it was as if, I thought, Amy was trying to recapture that northern land-scape where she had last seen Scupper, to go as far from the lush, semi-tropical setting of the garden and the river as it was possible to go. We walked through a thin fringe of trees and looked out at the old stones of the druids, tall as the fingers of a half-buried giant. The sky had produced a shaft of purplish light, which came down on the stones as if switched on by a master-surgeon to illuminate a petrified limb. I knew suddenly that I had no desire to hear Amy's confidences; that I wasn't ready for an intimacy which she had, after all, only last night refused me with a determined coolness. Yet although I wanted only to 'change the subject' – as Amy had often, giggling, said was her mother's favour-ite phrase if anything too 'personal' came up – I knew it would be wrong to do so. I gulped the upland air and watched a lark fly out of the short grass, to rise above the tall pines of the plateau. 'It's a chaffinch,' Amy said, amused, as if she could guess my urban romanticism and inaccuracy.

'And what about Candida,' I said, as if another species

of feathered friend had come as naturally into the conversation. 'I mean – at the waterfall –'

Amy shot me a quick glance. I felt already I shouldn't have spoken; and this not just because I wanted to protect myself. Yet she had moved a little away, over ground that was a fair imitation, in miniature, of that northern scene: heather and ling on a low escarpment, a dark, hard soil instead of grass, sprinkled with pine cones and rabbit-droppings. 'It's got nothing to do with Candida,' she said. She sounded impatient, but not annoyed. 'I was telling you – Daddy – well, he came and joined us there.'

'Oh, I see,' I said; and for some reason felt afraid, realizing now I would rather the tale of love for Scupper, his possible preference for Candida, than what was about to come. 'I mean I don't see,' I added, both as a spur and a way of putting an end to the conversation if Amy wished. She shrugged, increasing speed, now about six inches taller than I was as she walked the perimeter of the grassy atoll, I half running to keep up, below.

'You know, my father is a very kind man.' This was said in a fast, excited voice which made me dread even more the revelation of the trauma, for such, at the Mare's Tail, it must have been. 'Well, Jasmine – that silly Jasmine – she climbed up the side of the waterfall – and went right behind it. And got stuck.'

'Behind it?' Another vision, 'Thurberesque' as those friends of my Aunt Babs who had been recently introduced to the great American comic artist were already beginning to say, entered my mind and refused to go away. This was of the nude Jasmine Tremlett, 'curtain' of dark hair swinging, running behind another curtain, this time of fast-running water as it plunged down the gorge to a deep pool. 'There's a sort of cave half-way up, behind the . . .' Amy looked round at me and stopped. A smile spread over her face as well.

'The tail?' I said, beginning to laugh with relief, to feel the cold, strong gusts of air fill my lungs. We had come out at the southernmost end of the ridge by now, and stared down as if from the deck of a ship at the acres of gold stubble and dark wooded valleys of Lovescombe land. Lovegrove itself was hidden in a fold of the downs that looked as if it had been pulled up in an act of modesty to conceal it.

'My father rushed in to rescue her . . .'

'Behind the tail,' I said, choking with laughter now, unable to stop, falling forward into the pockets of wind, arms outstretched. Amy's laughter was carried away downwind, floating to the places where she had wandered – or so I felt – too often, brooding on her father's infidelity to her mother, and on her own loneliness. We laughed in a welcome return to childhood: a shared refusal to see yet the passions and complications of 'grown-up' life.

'Come on, Jenny,' Amy called out, as she leapt down the hill and then ran, zigzagging like a hare, to the green cleft at the bottom. 'Come on, Jenny. We're late. We'll go to the house by the Children's Garden.'

To look back on that day at Lovegrove – which, for many years I did, searching for the cause of my own blindness in the face of such an obvious set of circumstances, excusing myself on the grounds of youth and inexperience – is also to see that day, long and undulating, like the river which flows through the gardens of this exaggerated family, and which goes at last, after passing through a succession of artificial heights and pools, into the sea of ordinary, every-day life. The final episode, like Amy's attempt at explaining a level of sophisticated knowledge she almost certainly did not possess, was as ludicrous as the tale of the Mare's Tail, for Lovegrove – indeed anywhere belonging to the Loves-combe family – had, like a fatal inbuilt flaw, a predilection for the comic and absurd, sex, greed and flattery being, as in a Molière play, liable to 'bring down' the characters at any point. The extreme dignity of Lady Lovescombe pre-vented her, it seemed, from seeing this, so that the whole-sale expulsion of her daughter's friends at the end of that day had apparently no connection with her own surpris-ingly (to me) unconventional behaviour. An unease on this subject was not to be assuaged by Amy, who refused abso-lutely to see the actions of her parents and their friends in the light that I – or my Aunt Babs, say – were bound to see them, that is to say, highly questionable.

In this respect too I was glad to shoot the rapids of that day and, by the end of it, find myself back in the main-stream: in London, in the litter-strewn streets round Praed Street, the only escape into fantasy being that provided by the Gaumont, Notting Hill.

The first shock, which I came to think later had been purposely engineered by Amy (who was, I saw much later, trying to 'show' me, as with a succession of slides, or one of those early films in which the words are printed on the screen between 'takes', her understanding of her emotional background) was that of the Children's Garden and its occupants. It was more a case of 'double-take' perhaps, for after leaving the downs and crossing a narrow lane – a remembered link with the outside world (for it was along this road that I had come the day before: it seemed to have narrowed now, though, and to be hardly worth considering seriously as a way out) – we opened what Amy referred to as the 'wicket gate' and climbed up through rhododen-drons and laurel to the high ground above the house. Here there was a sort of tower or turret; and we peered through dank leaves at its base at a garden laid out with colour and formal precision. The height of the garden was approximately the same, I suppose, as 'Uncle Si's' raised garden with roses and hammock, and on that same ridge of land which hid both his house and Lovegrove from the open stare of the downs. At the time, the Edwardian concept of a garden specifically for children seemed to me charming rather than expressive of the desire, evident in architecture and in hierarchical institutions, for a policy of divide and rule, this policy coming, so to speak, to full fruit in the reign of Lord Lovescombe's father and grandfather. I saw only the delightful symmetry of the little box-bordered beds and the pear and apple trees along the walls, the beds filled with begonias, fuchsias and geraniums. Low iron gates opened at the far end of the garden, which was enclosed on two sides by tree-espaliered walls and on one side by the Tower, which seemed to have no purpose other than to be a sort of look-out post: spiral stone stairs went up from a ground floor that contained nothing but a stone bench, this much defaced by the scribblings of village children (or so it seemed: it was unlikely that the Lovescombes, however powerful their passions of the time, would engrave hearts and names on their own property). The fact that the garden had been screened off in this way from the house was of course symptomatic of the Lovescombe – or Edwardian – way of treating children: most of the time to be neither seen nor heard, but 'spoilt' with gifts, inheritances, gardens of their own. There was even a shallow pool in the middle of the garden into which a stone Cupid timelessly peed, a chubby leg and arm raised in the simulation of flight.

In the stone pool, floating white hair at first apparently the fronds of a water-lily or some such decorative piece of

Aesthetic Movement flora as would be deemed suitable by Lady Lovescombe for the adornment of this most sacred of founts, the pool with a garden dedicated to children, lay Lady Lovescombe herself. Her face was upturned and what Carmen would doubtless have referred to as her 'boobs', slightly muddied by the waters of the primitive pond, were visible above the water. Beside her, as unexpected a sight just as much for reasons of his supposed antipathy to water – the dirt and general hirsuteness of his appearance being hardly attributable to daily ablutions – swam Bernard Ehrlich. Arms flailing, the famous painter seemed to be making a good deal of his immersion in water, the energy of his actions suggesting, at the very least, an imminent drowning, this being a feat almost impossible in what was clearly no more than a toddler-height pool. For a moment it did occur to me that these motions had less to do with swimming than with some other form of activity which, although I was not personally familiar with it, had been glimpsed in a magazine once brought to Aunt Babs' house by the Brigadier and left inadvertently in his mackintosh pocket for the duration of lunch, a meal I finished before he did; this magazine being instantly confiscated by Aunt Babs when I was found looking through it in the bathroom, some instinct having told her that I was being 'rather quiet' and therefore perhaps not 'all right' – or even, in Aunt Babs' dread of my coming puberty, about to be 'unwell'. Certainly, the unusual attitudes of the men and women in the magazine had brought on a feeling of unwellness, although I was never able to say why, their actions being, presumably, completely natural. It was the frenetic expressions on their faces, I think, which caused alarm; this same eager and distanced look being, on nervous and second inspection, visible on the features of both Lady Lovescombe and Bernard Ehrlich, who were, nevertheless, too far apart to be making a 'beast with two backs', and, in the case of Ehrlich, merely trying to keep afloat. Amy gave a short laugh. There was a generally accepted idea, as I was to discover later, that the 'circle' of a woman like Lady Lovescombe – with her 'interest in the arts' and the furnishing and maintenance of her houses to keep her occupied – was considered likely to be 'queer' (the men of the circle, at least); and this Lord Lovescombe was to underline later in that disastrous day, even citing Ehrlich himself as 'queer', despite plenty of evidence, it would have seemed, to the contrary. This 'queerness', once implied, however, did somehow neutralize an otherwise explosive situation, and was clearly the tactic of a husband concerned that his spouse's chastity and artistic judgement were irreproachable (a stance which was sorely in need of justification, as I was to see on the occasion of the long-awaited visit to Lord Lovescombe's modern-art collection and Ehrlich's presentations of female nudity on show there).

'Hello, Mummy.' Amy had clearly witnessed the nude bathing of her mother and the famous painter before; had indeed witnessed worse, in the case of Jasmine Tremlett's naked cross-country dash from bamboo clump to house. I wondered how Amy planned to live her life when she was married. I wondered about this, I suppose, because I felt Amy's insecurity in the face of parents so adulterous and yet so apparently doting; and I hoped at least that Amy would have a 'quiet life', whatever that might be, and not suffer what I then, in my naïvety, considered the unhappiness of a 'bad' marriage, mutual dislike being the obvious reason the Lovescombes fell into the arms of their Bohemian friends. What shocked me too much, at that point, to see for myself, was that the Lovescombes were perfectly happy with their 'arrangement'; that as long as 'appearances' were kept up they felt free to do as they pleased; and that these 'appearances' must be believed by their own children, a situation likely to drive a child to the edge of insanity – particularly when accompanied, as it would if some true parental example had been on offer, by disciplinary measures, rewards and punishments for filial obedience and love. It was as if, I thought, still in my uneasy position at the edge of the laurel bushes a few feet from the pool, these 'devoted parents' must show they were recipients of love from every possible direction; like millionaires in a toy shop, they could acquire casual partners, marriage partners, 'lightning affairs' and children at will, all of these being expected, at the push of a button, to give evidence of affection and loyalty. I thought, too – but only years later, when that day was brought forcibly back to me by the sudden arrival of the white Chelsea dove on my Aunt Babs' stall, its beauty of line and glazed eye reminding me somehow of the toughness and fragility of Lady Lovescombe as she lay spreadeagled in the muddy waters of the pond in the Children's Garden – that this demand for her own children to 'look the other way' while giving proof of their belief in dedicated parental love, must be a factor in Amy's 'absences' when sitting or talking with one: as if 'looking away' had become a habit from early childhood; and accounting too for Amy's simple 'crush' on Scupper who, being unattached, could hardly impose these double standards on her. That Amy would suffer as a result of Scupper's attentions to Candida became a fear for me as we walked unseeingly (or pretended to) down the thin strip of grass between pond and bushes, averting our eyes from any possible appendages of Bernard Ehrlich that might have floated to the top – like onions in a stew – for the painter was now, in an effort to be more sure of not going under altogether, lying on his back.

I felt for Amy, in short, as I hadn't been able to do at

'Uncle Si's', where the burden of her inheritance, translated in her uncle's capering postures and mad harlequinade of the twenties, had been too much to bear, the sugared atmosphere poisoning my new friendship for her: I had been oppressed rather than impressed by the show. Now, though, I felt her vulnerable. Perhaps there had been a way in which she *had* tried to set out to impress me with the visit to 'Uncle Si's', like a schoolchild with superior possessions, and I had resented this, while, in the face of her defence-lessness, I was able to pity her. That she had deliberately stage-managed this I don't deny thinking – perhaps with an instinctive need for my compassion after the distancing effect of our earlier walk through the woods and into Sunset Boulevard. I had no further time for such considerations, however, as a figure, soon identifiable as Miss Bolt, was hurrying up the steps in the bank that led to our piece of raised ground, and opening the gate at the end of the Children's Garden.

'It's lunch in ten minutes, Lady Lovescombe.'

This announcement, which appeared to leave Lady Lovescombe unperturbed – she lifted a hand, I think, exposing her upper torso fully for a moment and then relapsed into the concealing water – had the opposite effect on Bernard Ehrlich, who sank suddenly from sight, only to bob up a few moments later in the middle of the pond, face ghastly and hair flattened to the side of his head by the constant stream of water from the chipped stone pudenda of the Cupid. I did then feel surprise, I must confess, at the love and keen rivalry felt by so many women for such a man but, though far from an expert on the dimensions of any males other than the petrified Pans of Kensington Gardens (or indeed, in the case of Lovegrove, this same Cupid whose proportions had most likely been played down in consideration of a site in a Children's Garden), I was able, as the painter reached full height, to gauge what must have been of compelling interest to them.

Miss Bolt, or 'Boltie', as Amy called her, was tugging at my sleeve and saying we must hurry to get ready for lunch. I do see now that Miss Bolt had glimpsed Ehrlich rising, a sallow Adonis, from the shallow waters of the Children's Garden pond, and was determined too late to save Amy and myself from the same experience: the information which followed this, though, that 'Lord Lovescombe went to the weir to meet you, Amy, and you weren't there, so he'll be glad to know you're back; you run and tell him, he's in the library,' being almost immediately negated by Lord Lovescombe's arrival at the gate to the garden and his bellowing shout to his wife on the subject of the luncheon arrangements.

I suppose my embarrassment at the confusion – for such, I thought, there must be – of a husband on finding his wife in the nude in a pond suitable for small children, with a man equally 'in the buff' as my Aunt Babs' unfailingly devoted and unrequited admirer the Brigadier would have put it, was misplaced: Amy, at least, seeming more annoyed by my shuffling feet and flaming cheeks than by the presumably acceptable state of affairs in which a cuckold calls out to his mate in full view of a member of his staff, not to mention the horn-supplier himself. Ehrlich subsided again quickly into the muddy waters, for I turned inadvertently – Amy not allowing me to leave the garden and Lord Lovescombe blocking the exit with his not inconsiderable bulk – to see only the ghastly face and flattened hair, like some mutant weed, afloat by the side of the pond. A hum of voices – at first I thought bees – came up from the lower levels of the Lovegrove gardens; this sound, I came to realize, being the approach of guests in large numbers. To my confusion was added shyness and the strongest desire I'd had yet to run off home again: a desire which, as I was hardly to know at the time, was to be granted before the end of the day. I dare say that if I'd known my stay was going to be severely curtailed, I would have found it possible to enjoy myself as an observer of a scene unlikely to be revisited in the foreseeable future; as it was, hearing the buzz of voices at the foot of the flight of wide steps to the 'bit of' garden where we stood, I felt only the vicarious mortification of those caught *in flagrante* – or, in the case of Lady Lovescombe, with whom I was for obvious reasons more likely to identify than with Ehrlich, the shame of Susanna regarded by the Elders; the shame being even greater in that Lady Lovescombe was, to my eyes at least, herself elderly. Whether to offer to run for a towel was, I felt, an unanswerable question, as the offer might be considered 'cheeky': that she might go uncovered to meet her guests was becoming, or so it seemed, inevitable; and, not being sure if she could hear the hum of the approaching guests through the sound of water busily made by the Cupid in the basin, I cleared my throat with a sound that brought further censure from the frowning Amy. All this, it proved, was unnecessary; also proving, I had to admit when I later looked back on my anxiety, an early symptom of becoming a 'worrier', as my Aunt Babs was. That Lady Lovescombe could 'look after herself' and had no need for me in her life to clothe or care for her was self-evident; that I found myself so closely concerned with what seemed to be her immediate problem was certainly mine. 'Boltie,' Lady Lovescombe called out. 'Bring me my robe, would you?'

This command seemed to release all of us on the stone surround by the pond – Lord Lovescombe backing out through the low gate to greet his guests, Amy and I tumbling after, and 'Boltie' literally flying, or such was the impression she gave in her downward flight to house and

robe, feet barely touching the steps – and we found ourselves meeting the assembled guests on a kind of wide
landing half-way between the stone flights; a landing taken
up with neat beds of lavender and an area of mown grass,
the smell from which gave a sudden poignancy to the
scene, this poignancy enhanced by the appearance of Mick
Scupper as he rose towards us. As Lord Lovescombe went
forward with outstretched hand, Amy shrank back against
me and whispered that we 'should get out of here'. Indeed,
as I saw from the vigorous nodding of her head, we could
retrace our footsteps, skirt the Children's Garden and come
down again into the lower, ornamental gardens of Lovegrove without having to penetrate the small crowd now
collecting on the grassy landing: the only problem was in
understanding why Amy should have become so unlike
her usual (in company at least) confident self. That she was
'bashful' in the presence of Scupper I decided must be the
reason (given my own fantasies on the subject of Ludo, I
was forced to admit I might become very bashful indeed if
he were suddenly to materialize), and that she had every
reason to wish to avoid Candida I could and did accept. Yet
– probably from a strong desire not to revisit the Children's
Garden – I chose to pretend not to be able to understand
Amy's violent head-shakings and stayed firmly rooted to
the spot. As might have been predicted, Candida rose with
the same smiling grace as Mick Scupper from the lower
ranges of the garden and came straight over to us. 'Amy!
Where on earth did you both go?'

Amy looked furiously at me in answer to this. My own
fascination with Lord Lovescombe's mode of greeting the
guests (of which there were only three newcomers, the
others being made up of Cranes, Tremletts and, in a freshly
ironed smock on which the daub of paint seemed to have
been consciously placed by a designer, Walter Neet)

distracted me from coming to the rescue. The greeting, in the case of a black-haired and unshaven new guest, comprised a kind of double grip whereby the host seemed to be pulling off the lower arm of the recent arrival while securing the upper arm just below the elbow with his 'free' hand. 'Jack!' Lord Lovescombe repeated several times, while a woman, presumably the dark man's wife, stood patiently, waiting her turn. 'Jack,' Lord Lovescombe continued, intending, as it finally became clear, to include the wife in this, 'jolly good to see you both!'

Behind the couple stood a boy of about eighteen. It was his evident contempt for the scene, it came to me fleetingly, that might have so affected Amy. The boy glowered and as Lord Lovescombe, who had indeed decided – or so it appeared – to include this new family, like a flag that has suddenly and unexpectedly been raised, under the one name of Jack, now suggested 'going down to the house for a snifter', it was impossible to know either his name or the reason for his anger.

'You must have been travelling for some time,' Lord Lovescombe remarked to the dark man, in a tone that showed mild surprise. 'Came from Shaftesbury, did you?'

The new guest, having given no sign of accepting that his name was Jack, was evidently not going to disclose his provenance, and if it hadn't been for Miss Bolt we might have stayed there indefinitely, Lord Lovescombe showing no sign of being prepared to move down towards the anticipated drinks until his guest had vouchsafed from which direction he and his family had come. Miss Bolt, however, released us once more; and to my considerable relief, I must say, my position there having become increasingly untenable. This was due to certain movements, 'brushings against', I suppose they could be called, made by Mick Scupper against Amy; and these ran, as if some electric current had been set off in the process, through her body into mine, the two of us being closely pressed together in the limited space available on the garden steps. Candida, on the other side of Scupper, must have been a recipient as well, of these (to her, because made to the wrong person) distinctly unwelcome advances. For me, the obvious distaste occasioned by experiencing Mick Scupper at, so to speak, one remove was made all the more unpalatable by the sight of Carmen, closely followed by Sonia Fount and casually swinging her 'bucket' bag, coming up towards us from the house. Remembering Carmen's capacity for violent revenge soon became the sole reason for staying close to Candida and Amy, in the hope that the three of us would form a sort of Parthenon through which Carmen would be unable to see Bernard Ehrlich rise from the pond at the top of the garden; luckily, however, the tide turned against her and we all began a serious descent of the steps, the scowling young man directing, as we went, a particularly vehement look in the direction of Amy.

CHAPTER
THIRTEEN

There may, in some romantic stories, be a moment when a future husband, glimpsed and dimly recognized in childhood, imparts a sense of mystery and excitement to a scene; but this was certainly not the case on the occasion of the visit of J. D. Hare, novelist and cousin (through the Azebys: 'a black Azeby' as Walter Neet remarked after lunch, while on our way through the house to the promised treasures of the Modern Art Collection); Hare being the father of the scowling Crispin who was to become the husband of Amy four years later. If this sounds synoptic, it is probably because there is always something unlikely, operatic, about the marriage of young people who appear to have come together for reasons of plot (in this case their parents) and who have nothing in common – though conceivably there is not much to have in common anyway at so early a stage. The element of chance always inherent in a marriage seems almost painfully stressed. That Amy and Crispin Hare were related was a factor to which I should have paid more attention, I now realize. At the time of the unpropitious lunch, however, if a *frisson* existed between the youthful cousins it was certainly one of mutual dread (I was to discover from Amy that Lady Lovescombe and Mrs Hare were always 'throwing them together' and that they had undergone the indignity, in the last holidays, of visiting the Curzon Cinema alone together, to see the latest film by Jacques Tati. That this had been a disaster was reflected in the fact that no one at school had heard about the 'date' and it was only as we split off from the pre-luncheon crowd at Lovegrove and ran on the lawn to go into the house through the drawing-room french window (now forever placed in my mind as a frame for the Giacometti-esque figure of Jasmine Tremlett) that Amy, spluttering at the memory of the dinner after the film at the 'Normandie Grill; disgusting, and it cost £3, which Daddy insisted on paying in advance', showed the extent of the humiliation imposed on her by her family). And I was to think, on the day in the Portobello Road when Carmen's dove 'turned up' on the stall – and a familiar figure, easily identifiable as Mick Scupper, appeared out of the crowd to inquire its price – of the refuge Amy must think she had found in marrying the young man of her parents' choice (the wedding invitation had arrived a couple of days before the surprise arrival of the dove and since Amy's 'coming out ball' – a fiasco at which Scupper had proved once again elusive – we had lost touch). Perhaps she felt she had come as close as someone so ineradicably stamped by a succession of inherited childhoods at Lovegrove could possibly come, to an independent life suitable for a woman who would marry and have to fend for herself. That she didn't have to fend for herself, of course, was another element I should have taken into account after the initial expression of surprise at the wedding invitation, Lord Lovescombe having 'set up' his young relative in a small business shortly after his eighteenth birthday; indeed, just before his visit to Lovegrove with his parents. It was this fact, possibly, which, if known only to Lord Lovescombe himself at the time, may have been in some way guessed by Amy, while the consequences attendant on it caused the antipathy expressed by the young Crispin; for certainly the marriage, over which I was to suffer such agonies of indecision, in the choice of wedding present and suitable outfit, hardly lasted longer than my own feelings of surprise and confusion.

Whatever the future might hold, lunch that day at Love-grove was undeniably as 'difficult' as the guest-list might lead one to expect, the presence of J. D. Hare and his wife and son doing little other than add to the general feeling of constraint and – for no reason that I could make out – a sort of muffled indignation, as if the richness of the food and the sameness of the dining-room could hardly be repeated so soon after last night's dinner of spilt grouse and this morning's breakfast. Lady Lovescombe, who appeared just as the guests had been served with sherry in the drawing-room, her (presumably still wet) hair concealed by a 'taste-ful' scarf of crisp blue cotton, seemed out of sorts: bad-tempered even. It crossed my mind that the presence of Carmen and Sonia Fount – who had not been fully expected, as I was to realize on going through the dining-room to fetch a tomato juice for Mrs Hare ('It's in the pantry – no point in ringing for Vine,' Lord Lovescombe had said in tones of equal bad temper) – to find Vine adding two places to the 'spare' table at the end of the room overlooking the bamboo clump most recently a shelter for Jasmine Tremlett – it crossed my mind, as I say, that Lady Loves-combe, despite her (to me) almost frighteningly advanced years, might be jealous of Ehrlich's retinue and out of sorts at the prospect of an afternoon spent in their company, while Lord Lovescombe, delegated to showing his cousin the novelist ancestral portraits from which the 'black Azebys' doubtless originated, would equally find imposs-ible the sating of his (I by now imagined) insatiable lust in the bamboo clump below. Amy, who had as cross a face as either of her parents now we were inside the house away from the grassy landing where Scupper had pressed his knee on hers, was undergoing the further humiliation of looking around for him and seeing him nowhere, while Candida's 'demure' expression was reminiscent of those occasions at school when she received a compliment from the English teacher. To spare Amy further agony I went over and took Candida aside, hoping against hope, perhaps, that what seemed to be the inevitable outcome of this farcical 'old-girls' reunion might still be prevented from taking place.

'What do you want?' I was reminded for a moment of the end of an English lesson at St Peter's when, the drama-mistress having left and Candida's smirks for preferment for a major role being no longer necessary, she rounded on the other girls and snapped at them to make a neat pile of their copies of *The Merchant of Venice*.

'I just . . .' I faltered, seeing a look in Candida I hadn't seen before: the boa constrictor in the throes of a romantic, passionate love. The skin had tightened to a point of blueness under the chin and a triangular shape, a face with a falling 'quiff' of hair, danced in the pupils of her eyes. 'I mean . . .' I went on, knowing I sounded desperate, 'I wanted to ask you about Castle Azeby.'

Candida looked at me as if I had just been certified insane and then handed into her custody for the unforeseeable future. 'What about it?' It was hard to tell, from the scorn in her voice, whether a knowledge of all aspects of the Lovescombe family was, like the Michelin Guide to a gourmet, a prerequisite for civilized life, or whether, like some Rosicrucian secret, Castle Azeby and its inner workings were for the initiated only, a group which I, coming late and a *parvenue* to Amy's circle, had no right to join. After a while, however, Candida pursed her lips prior to parting them and, speaking in her usual clipped, sibilant manner, said, 'Ludo loves it more than anywhere in the world.'

This statement, overlaid as it was by the sudden eruption into the room of Victor Crane, managed nevertheless to re-awaken the longings for Ludo which I had – I must suppose – hoped would never stir in me again, the 'hopeless passion' side of it all being accentuated by Ludo's overriding love for a place I had never even seen, a rival superior to any woman – like hearing from the lips of Emily Brontë that Heathcliff had really all along loved Wuthering Heights a great deal more than Catherine. 'It's his now, you know,' added Candida primly (and for a moment, I admit, my heart sank at the vision of her ensconced there, mistress of Castle Azeby, pouring out tea in a library 'swept down on' by moors; this sinking of the heart proving, as with some, if not all of my 'hunches' on that day at Lovegrove, to be not as far from the truth as I might have hoped). 'It's . . .' Candida paused for reflection, as if the size of the castle and estate could hardly be conveyed with a vulgar gesture such as an unfurling of arms. 'There's a drawbridge . . .'

At this point both Victor Crane and Walter Neet, who had changed out of his smock and into a suit of vomit-coloured hound's-tooth, came up together: glad, I thought, of an opportunity to impress Candida – and possibly even myself – though the previous evening's encounters with both had, from any point of view, been highly unsuccess-ful.

'Castle Azeby – did I hear you say Castle Azeby?' Neet peered anxiously at Candida, as if she had indeed given away a fairly important and confidential piece of infor-mation. Amalia Drifton, who had eschewed her brother's sherry and was, I saw with some apprehension, 'nursing' a beaker of dry martini in which a scrap of lemon floated like the victim of some marine disaster, stared angrily at our group, her family home (or one of them) being possibly a private matter between herself and the building. I began to wonder about the place, seeing Lovegrove as a decadent, southerly seat for a family who should have stayed in the north in the first place, guarding the fortune made there and remaining, if necessary, permanently behind the drawbridge, not admitting such people as Walter Neet, Victor Crane – or, indeed, myself. 'In my room I have a recent oil of Castle Azeby,' Walter Neet vouchsafed, this news in itself risky-sounding, particularly in view of Amalia Drifton bearing down on us, as she was at that moment doing, martini held high like some advertisement for 'high and dry' possibly, or in order not to jog her niece. 'I suggest you come and see it now,' Neet added; then, seeing my look of alarm, and remembering, more than likely, his keyhole scenes of the evening before, he went on at greater speed, 'Time for a little party to be got up. See old Richard's collection of modern art after lunch, see mine first.'

'How many properties amount to a monopoly?' Victor Crane put in here in a bright, facetious tone slightly surprising, I confess, as his 'crumpled look' from the night before, much in evidence at breakfast, had by no means worn off. I wondered, even, if the imminent arrival of Amalia Drifton's raised beaker had, like a hare to a hound, set off some complex chain reaction whereby he would get 'roaring drunk' (an expression I had heard his wife use, in accusing him, the night before, of taking too much port in his chair under the gentle and reproving eye of Lady Azeby) at one remove. This did indeed seem to be the case, as Crane, spotting Amalia and the gin, let out a roar of welcome far exceeding his presumed acquaintance with her: causing indeed a fine rain of martini to fall on the head of Walter Neet, himself by now a regular receptacle for dropped food and drink when staying with the Lovescombes. 'I'm so sorry,' Amalia Drifton said with a vague expression of distaste, though whether she was sorry at the loss of some of the precious spirit on Neet's oiled white thatch, or for the old painter himself was not clear. 'I heard you talking about Castle Azeby, I believe?'

'I was only suggesting,' Neet replied, on the defensive now and still standing, owing to the congestion in this part of the drawing-room, directly under the drip; 'only suggesting that an expedition might be mounted in order to view my recent oil of the castle and grounds . . .'

'Excuse me.' Bernard Ehrlich – face so startlingly white that it seemed the immersion in the pond in the Children's Garden must, paradoxically, have washed off some of the dirt, like a sparrow's dustbath perhaps, or the healing mud of a spa – brushed past on his way to the door, where Carmen and Sonia Fount, who had now been joined by 'Boltie', were standing; Sonia Fount with the look of hauteur which was a result, as I was told by Candida on the long journey home later that night, of the immense fortune into which she had been born; Carmen with a look of nonchalance scarcely believable in view of the 'swag' still tucked away in the bag now hanging loosely over her shoulder. 'Boltie', meanwhile, was clearly trying to announce that luncheon was ready, a task normally undertaken by Vine but this time handed over to the amanuensis (as the Brigadier decided she must be, in his long examination of the hierarchy of Lovegrove, details of which were demanded for many months after the end of my suddenly truncated visit).

'Little swine!' Walter Neet appeared at first to be addressing himself, until a violent jerk of the head in Ehrlich's rapidly vanishing direction showed that the old artist held the latest fashion in art in low esteem. 'Fraud! Have you *seen* his work . . .' Here Neet searched gallantly for my name and then gave up. 'Jane . . . I mean have you tried to stand in front of a canvas of that fellow's without actually being sick?'

As Neet's own hound's-tooth apparel seemed to suggest a recent visit to Ehrlich's works – to purge himself of envy for Ehrlich's greater fame perhaps, or to regain confidence at least in the 'old, time-honoured way' of representing reality (the Brigadier again; much to my Aunt Babs' disapproval) – I judged it best to say nothing about my 'connection' with Ehrlich, which was of course Carmen. There was unfortunately no need for my reticence, however, as Neet now very deliberately drew me aside, leaving Victor Crane and Amalia Drifton, the glass with the remains of the intoxicating beverage between them like some kind of Biblical chalice, staring wordlessly into each other's faces. 'You see . . . Jane . . . I've got to tell you this. I hope you won't mind . . . indeed I know you won't mind . . . I do so need your understanding in this.'

Miss Bolt's intervention, miraculous as always, didn't on this occasion, however, prevent Walter Neet from going on. 'Lunch is served, Lady Lovescombe,' went unheard by nearly all the guests, and certainly by Lady Lovescombe, who was over by the french window with Mrs Hare, telling her, I thought, about Jasmine's extraordinary daring the evening before when she had been seen naked in the close vicinity (though on second thoughts this seemed improbable; and with the benefit of hindsight was more likely to consist of shared confidences on the subject of their children, whose marriage had been implicitly arranged when they were still in the cradle). Neet, less willing to hear the announcement of lunch than most, pressed closer, this movement freeing Candida and enabling her to rejoin Amy, which in turn raised an ironic cheer from Carmen, always the first to notice what she would call 'shenanigans' in the offing. Neet, on hearing the cheer, turned to the door and back again to me, his expression darkened, or so it seemed, with an unmistakable misery. 'It's Carmen,' he said, when it was ascertained that neither Crane nor Amalia Drifton were listening, the ill-assorted pair having got into a half-hearted bickering over the private ownership of land.

'Carmen?' I was aware of looking bemused; I was hungry, too, as the call for food went unheeded. 'Why Carmen?'

'I've fallen in love.' The elderly painter faced me square on; at the same time a loud gong thundered from the hall. I began to move sideways as unobtrusively as possible, guessing that with such large numbers we would help ourselves rather than be waited on by Vine; and that it would be very much first come, first served, with the food possibly in short supply, given the unexpected presence of what Jim Tremlett was heard to call 'Bernard Ehrlich's nereids'. 'Hopelessly in love,' Neet continued, in what he must have thought was a whisper, a sort of mild stampede for lunch having started up in the drawing-room at the sound of the gong. 'But why should it all be so hopeless? After all, Talleyrand had an affair with his niece, who was a good sixty years younger.'

On looking back at the remainder of that day, I think it's the figure of Miss Bolt, in the end, that stands out: 'Boltie' as messenger, spy, interfering angel in the house. In an attempt to escape the continued attentions of Walter Neet (for now that I was his confidante he had taken an Ancient Mariner position, reciting instances of other ancients with their protégées and recounting several times how Carmen had smiled at him on the upper corridor before lunch – I wondered what she had been doing there, on hearing this, and decided I would rather not think about it) I followed Miss Bolt into the dining-room and over to the 'Children's Table' laid at the end, an obvious placing for invisible people such as Amy's friends, and indeed for Miss Bolt herself.

Neet, seeing that his idol had no intention of joining us – for one moment I thought Carmen might go right next to Lord Lovescombe, laying her bag with its bird at his feet while she helped herself to her portion of beef – Neet at least, on seeing her join the main table ('plonk yourself down,' Lord Lovescombe shouted, indicating with a point-ing finger three chairs which would accommodate Ehrlich and his retinue) shuffled over and sat with them, much to my relief. A parade of would-be lunchers then approached the side-table, with its hotplate and array of roast and boiled potatoes, vegetable dishes and salad bowl, and stood behind Lord Lovescombe as he applied himself to carving the joint. The long walk of the morning to 'Uncle Si's', followed by the trek over the ridge below Stonehenge and the return through the Children's Garden to the house, had made me faint with hunger, and I watched apprehen-sively as slivers of beef – 'overdone as usual' I heard Amalia Drifton mutter in the direction of Lady Lovescombe – were slipped on to plates. A side of cold ham, clearly placed there at the last moment by Vine in an attempt to assuage the panic of the guests, seemed to look more and more necess-ary. It was even offered, I saw, to Victor Crane, on the understanding, most probably, that it would make little difference what he ate, alcohol and Communism being pre-sumed to have long ago destroyed his taste buds.

'I'll have the beef, Richard, if I may.' Crane was now at the head of the queue; J. D. Hare, an equally shambling figure, stood just behind him. I feared, I must admit, for the future of the lunch altogether if both men were to succumb to what the Brigadier referred to as the 'high intake' (referring in this case to my Aunt Babs' friend Ethyl, who had been known to come for a teatime visit and 'kill' a bottle of sherry). 'Roast beef of England,' Crane added, with an odd, persecuted glint in his eye, as if teaching a member of the Comintern the commodities he would be wise to order when next spying for his country on these shores. 'I say – I do beg your pardon . . .'

The worst, though it might well have been imagined by the tone of Victor Crane's apology, succeeded by his wife's drawn-out hiss of, 'For God's sake, Victor,' was not in fact the fall of the sirloin of beef from the already strangely unsteady carving-table. Crane, crowding closer to see his coming lunch, and embarking on an anecdote of a Tory squire who had recently intimated to him that England would shortly be taken over by his private army (though it was hard to see who these confidants of Crane's could be): 'We have the beef and we have the bullets,' Crane had just cried; 'that's what the brave bart said to me,' had perhaps mistaken the whiteness of the sauce for the tablecloth and placed his hand palm down in a dish of horseradish, withdrawing it with a look of abject fear.

'How absolutely awful,' Amalia Drifton said loudly, and then returned to her conversation with Lady Lovescombe (heard only too easily by me, as my end of the queue, not even yet at the point when it would join the 'grown-up' one, was next to Lady Lovescombe by the Children's Table at the bay window looking out over the garden). 'I mean, they have so *little* money,' Amalia Drifton went on, showing as she spoke that Crane's sudden anointment with the horseradish had not been the reason for her scathing comment, 'so terribly little, I've heard.'

Lady Lovescombe looked mysterious at this; for a moment the sisters-in-law stood close together and seemed, as the Brigadier would have put it, to be 'in cahoots'. Something to do with money and with the 'poor Hares' was muttered and Amalia Drifton gave a short grunt of approval: I, of course, was oblivious to the meaning of all this until many years later, when the gossip column of a popular newspaper read and recited from by the Brigadier informed us that 'the groom, Mr Crispin Hare, is managing director of Hare, Lovescombe and Rudd, an insurance company recently set up in the City'; nor, I may say, did I at that particular time have any concept whatsoever of the importance of money to a family such as Amy's, the suggestion, in fact, being that Lovegrove was a treasure-house for works of art too priceless to be connected in any way with the market-place: stored there, overseen by the Lovescombes in their lifetime but otherwise, in some way too nebulous to explain, the property of the nation. I was wrong about this, which became clear as I grew older, though Aunt Babs' own unworldly stance on these matters was little training for 'the jungle' (Crane's term, said excitedly when 'Big Money' was mentioned and giving the impression that, although it went against his principles, the jungle was a more lively place to find yourself than on the plains of the Five Year Plan). That money was the very pigment that ran through the pictures at Lovegrove, the cement of the fairytale construction, was undoubtedly true. I dare say, too, that my own preoccupation with Ludo had made me more foolish than usual when it came to the realities of life. And that Amy was included in Lady Lovescombe's conversation with her sister-in-law on the subject of the Hares should have been obvious. At that age, however, an uneasy feeling – which I most certainly suffered in that interminable wait for the roast beef – can easily be mistaken for social malaise or simple shyness, which a room full of hardly-known people is likely to impart, so I paid more attention to the expression on Amy's face, this seeming to warrant more concern.

Amy was sitting at the main table, only 'Boltie', Mary Crane and I, it seemed, having gone meekly to the Children's Table at the end of the room. Possibly she had wanted to keep an eye on Carmen – or had vaguely suspected the bucket bag – but she wanted, I realized with a sudden sense of agitation, to keep an eye on Candida even more. And Candida – however much one might look round the room and at the clusters of guests – was not there. I saw that Amy, too, was looking for her. As I edged up towards Lord Lovescombe and the carving-knife, I scanned the room with the kind of impatience a theatre-goer feels when the curtain fails to go up. The play, of course, for which we were waiting (and which no one wanted to see) being the betrayal of Amy by Candida: the first treacherous step to womanhood.

CHAPTER FOURTEEN

I should have known, I suppose, that the 'shenanigans' prophesied by a delighted Carmen (on noting the absence of Candida and Scupper she came briskly over to me, leaving her bag dangling over the back of one of the Chippendale dining chairs of which Lord Lovescombe was so proud and, rolling her eyes, remarked that now the 'cat would be in among the pigeons') were of no real interest to Amy. I should have thought then, too, rather than later, of the signs and implications, inherent in family life at Lovegrove, which I had myself failed to picture on my short visit there. From the time at lunch when Amalia Drifton, sharp-eyed as ever, remarked that 'that little friend of Amy's and the art bloke have gone astray', to 'Boltie's' successful search for the missing couple (who were found, it transpired, at the top of the winding stairs in the turret of the Children's Garden – an assignation made, presumably, by Scupper and Candida on the grassy landing – where he had gone, one had to suppose, early, to sit among the graffiti and entwined hearts, thus avoiding being seen publicly leaving the dining-room), was a matter of a mere half-hour, between the clearing of the Yorkshire pudding and the arrival of the Bakewell tart.

It was Carmen, however, who brought things into

perspective – for me, at least – as we stood in Walter Neet's bedroom for an after-lunch 'viewing': a flatulent, unwilling crowd, just 'subjected' (as most of the audience would see it) to the works of Nash, Piper, Keith Vaughan, Sutherland, Victor Pasmore and others; and 'not quite the right moment for this just after lunch' as Amalia Drifton was heard to remark, also to the various carcasses of Bernard Ehrlich. That these included Lady Lovescombe and Jasmine Tremlett was painfully obvious, the naked, in some cases flayed, flesh occasioning Lord Lovescombe's muffled assertions that Ehrlich was 'as queer as a coot'.

We stood looking at Neet's representation of a murky scene in a great park, autumn leaves painstakingly scattered on the ground and a boy and girl – just recognizably Amy and Ludo – standing inside the porch of a castle so vast as to disappear out of the top of the canvas altogether. In the picture Amy, who is leaning lightly against the roughly hewn stone wall, is dressed as if for a dance, despite the gloomy weather and general lack of jollity in the scene. Her dress is pink and light, like a ballerina's, while Ludo is in plus-fours and holding a gun. If it hadn't been for Carmen's laugh, and her remark that there's 'nothing like kicking off a shoe to feel at home', I don't think I'd have noticed Amy's slippers, pink satin to match her dress, among the leaves in the foreground; and I thought, though I was eager not to think of it, of the night before when I had roamed the house at Lovegrove and come down the back stairs to find Ludo – and the old nursery sofa – and a kicked-off pink satin shoe on the floor by the fire. 'The children,' Walter Neet continued, although his makeshift studio had now emptied of all but Amalia Drifton (eye roaming for spilt paint or vanished pieces of porcelain), Carmen and myself. 'The children have come out particularly well, in this one, don't you think?'

FOR THE BEST IN PAPERBACKS, LOOK FOR THE

In every corner of the world, on every subject under the sun, Penguin represents quality and variety – the very best in publishing today.

For complete information about books available from Penguin – including Pelicans, Puffins, Peregrines and Penguin Classics – and how to order them, write to us at the appropriate address below. Please note that for copyright reasons the selection of books varies from country to country.

In the United Kingdom: For a complete list of books available from Penguin in the U.K., please write to *Dept E.P., Penguin Books Ltd, Harmondsworth, Middlesex, UB7 0DA*

In the United States: For a complete list of books available from Penguin in the U.S., please write to *Dept BA, Penguin, 299 Murray Hill Parkway, East Rutherford, New Jersey 07073*

In Canada: For a complete list of books available from Penguin in Canada, please write to *Penguin Books Canada Ltd, 2801 John Street, Markham, Ontario L3R 1B4*

In Australia: For a complete list of books available from Penguin in Australia, please write to the *Marketing Department, Penguin Books Australia Ltd, P.O. Box 257, Ringwood, Victoria 3134*

In New Zealand: For a complete list of books available from Penguin in New Zealand, please write to the *Marketing Department, Penguin Books (NZ) Ltd, Private Bag, Takapuna, Auckland 9*

In India: For a complete list of books available from Penguin, please write to *Penguin Overseas Ltd, 706 Eros Apartments, 56 Nehru Place, New Delhi, 110019*

In Holland: For a complete list of books available from Penguin in Holland, please write to *Penguin Books Nederland B.V., Postbus 195, NL–1380AD Weesp, Netherlands*

In Germany: For a complete list of books available from Penguin, please write to *Penguin Books Ltd, Friedrichstrasse 10 – 12, D–6000 Frankfurt Main 1, Federal Republic of Germany*

In Spain: For a complete list of books available from Penguin in Spain, please write to *Longman Penguin España, Calle San Nicolas 15, E–28013 Madrid, Spain*

A CHOICE OF PENGUIN FICTION

Monsignor Quixote Graham Greene

Now filmed for television, Graham Greene's novel, like Cervantes's seventeenth-century classic, is a brilliant fable for its times. 'A deliciously funny novel' – *The Times*

The Dearest and the Best Leslie Thomas

In the spring of 1940 the spectre of war turned into grim reality – and for all the inhabitants of the historic villages of the New Forest it was the beginning of the most bizarre, funny and tragic episode of their lives. 'Excellent' – *Sunday Times*

Earthly Powers Anthony Burgess

Anthony Burgess's magnificent masterpiece, an enthralling, epic narrative spanning six decades and spotlighting some of the most vivid events and characters of our times. 'Enormous imagination and vitality . . . a huge book in every way' – Bernard Levin in the *Sunday Times*

The Penitent Isaac Bashevis Singer

From the Nobel Prize-winning author comes a powerful story of a man who has material wealth but feels spiritually impoverished. 'Singer . . . restates with dignity the spiritual aspirations and the cultural complexities of a lifetime, and it must be said that in doing so he gives the Evil One no quarter and precious little advantage' – Anita Brookner in the *Sunday Times*

Paradise Postponed John Mortimer

'Hats off to John Mortimer. He's done it again' – *Spectator*. A rumbustious, hilarious new novel from the creator of Rumpole, *Paradise Postponed* was made into a major Thames Television series.

The Balkan Trilogy and Levant Trilogy Olivia Manning

'The finest fictional record of the war produced by a British writer. Her gallery of personages is huge, her scene painting superb, her pathos controlled, her humour quiet and civilized' – *Sunday Times*

A CHOICE OF PENGUIN FICTION

Maia   Richard Adams

The heroic romance of love and war in an ancient empire from one of our greatest storytellers. 'Enormous and powerful' – *Financial Times*

The Warning Bell   Lynne Reid Banks

A wonderfully involving, truthful novel about the choices a woman must make in her life – and the price she must pay for ignoring the counsel of her own heart. 'Lynne Reid Banks knows how to get to her reader: this novel grips like Super Glue' – *Observer*

Doctor Slaughter   Paul Theroux

Provocative and menacing – a brilliant dissection of lust, ambition and betrayal in 'civilized' London. 'Witty, chilly, exuberant, graphic' – *The Times Literary Supplement*. Now filmed as *Half Moon Street*.

Wise Virgin   A. N. Wilson

Giles Fox's work on the Pottle manuscript, a little-known thirteenth-century tract on virginity, leads him to some innovative research on the subject that takes even his breath away. 'A most elegant and chilling comedy' – *Observer* Books of the Year

Last Resorts   Clare Boylan

Harriet loved Joe Fisher for his ordinariness – for his ordinary suits and hats, his ordinary money and his ordinary mind, even for his ordinary wife. 'An unmitigated delight' – *Time Out*

Trade Wind   M. M. Kaye

An enthralling blend of history, adventure and romance from the author of the bestselling *The Far Pavilions*

A CHOICE OF PENGUIN FICTION

The Ghost Writer   Philip Roth

Philip Roth's celebrated novel about a young writer who meets and falls in love with Anne Frank in New England – or so he thinks. 'Brilliant, witty and extremely elegant' – *Guardian*

Small World   David Lodge

Shortlisted for the 1984 Booker Prize, *Small World* brings back Philip Swallow and Maurice Zapp for a jet-propelled journey into hilarity. 'The most brilliant and also the funniest novel that he has written' – *London Review of Books*

Treasures of Time   Penelope Lively

Beautifully written, acutely observed, and filled with Penelope Lively's sharp but compassionate wit, *Treasures of Time* explores the relationship between the lives we live and the lives we think we live.

Absolute Beginners   Colin MacInnes

The first 'teenage' novel, the classic of youth and disenchantment, *Absolute Beginners* is part of MacInnes's famous London trilogy – and now a brilliant film. 'MacInnes caught it first – and best' – *Harpers and Queen*

July's People   Nadine Gordimer

Set in South Africa, this novel gives us an unforgettable look at the terrifying, tacit understanding and misunderstandings between blacks and whites. 'This is the best novel that Miss Gordimer has ever written' – Alan Paton in the *Saturday Review*

The Ice Age   Margaret Drabble

'A continuously readable, continuously surprising book . . . here is a novelist who is not only popular and successful but formidably growing towards real stature' – *Observer*

A CHOICE OF PENGUIN FICTION

Money Martin Amis

Savage, audacious and demonically witty – a story of urban excess. 'Terribly, terminally funny: laughter in the dark, if ever I heard it' – *Guardian*

Lolita Vladimir Nabokov

Shot through with Nabokov's mercurial wit, quicksilver prose and intoxicating sensuality, *Lolita* is one of the world's great love stories. 'A great book' – Dorothy Parker

Dinner at the Homesick Restaurant Anne Tyler

Through every family run memories which bind them together – in spite of everything. 'She is a witch. Witty, civilized, curious, with her radar ears and her quill pen dipped on one page in acid and on the next in orange liqueur . . . a wonderful writer' – John Leonard in *The New York Times*

Glitz Elmore Leonard

Underneath the Boardwalk, a lot of insects creep. But the creepiest of all was Teddy. 'After finishing *Glitz*, I went out to the bookstore and bought everything else of Elmore Leonard I could find' – Stephen King

The Battle of Pollocks Crossing J. L. Carr

Shortlisted for the Booker McConnell Prize, this is a moving, comic masterpiece. 'Wayward, ambiguous, eccentric . . . a fascinatingly outlandish novel' – *Guardian*

The Dreams of an Average Man Dyan Sheldon

Tony Rivera is lost. Sandy Grossman Rivera is leaving. And Maggie Kelly is giving up. In the steamy streets of summertime Manhattan, the refugees of the sixties generation wonder what went wrong. 'Satire, dramatic irony and feminist fun . . . lively, forceful and funny' – *Listener*

A CHOICE OF PENGUIN FICTION

The Enigma of Arrival   V. S. Naipaul

'For sheer abundance of talent, there can hardly be a writer alive who surpasses V. S. Naipaul. Whatever we may want in a novelist is to be found in his books . . .' Irving Howe in *The New York Times Book Review*. 'Naipaul is always brilliant' – Anthony Burgess in the *Observer*

Only Children   Alison Lurie

When the Hubbards and the Zimmerns go to visit Anna on her idyllic farm, it becomes increasingly difficult to tell which are the adults, and which the children. 'It demands to be read' – *Financial Times*. 'There quite simply is no better living writer' – John Braine

My Family and Other Animals   Gerald Durrell

Gerald Durrell's wonderfully comic account of his childhood years on Corfu and his development as a naturalist and zoologist. Soaked in Greek sunshine, it is a 'bewitching book' – *Sunday Times*

Getting it Right   Elizabeth Jane Howard

A hairdresser in the West End, Gavin is sensitive, shy, into the arts, prone to spots and, at thirty-one, a virgin. He's a classic late developer – and maybe it's getting too late to develop at all? 'Crammed with incidental pleasures . . . sometimes sad but more frequently hilarious . . . *Getting it Right* gets it, comically, right' – Paul Bailey in the *London Standard*

The Vivisector   Patrick White

In this prodigious novel about the life and death of a great painter, Patrick White, winner of the Nobel Prize for Literature, illuminates creative experience with unique truthfulness. 'One of the most interesting and absorbing novelists writing in English today' – Angus Wilson in the *Observer*

The Echoing Grove   Rosamund Lehmann

'No English writer has told of the pains of women in love more truly or more movingly than Rosamund Lehmann' – Marghanita Laski 'She uses words with the enjoyment and mastery with which Renoir used paint' – Rebecca West in the *Sunday Times*. 'A magnificent achievement' – John Connell in the *Evening News*

A CHOICE OF PENGUIN FICTION

Other Women   Lisa Alther

From the bestselling author of *Kinflicks* comes this compelling novel of today's woman – and a heroine with whom millions of women will identify.

Your Lover Just Called   John Updike

Stories of Joan and Richard Maple – a couple multiplied by love and divided by lovers. Here is the portrait of a modern American marriage in all its mundane moments and highs and lows of love as only John Updike could draw it.

Mr Love and Justice   Colin MacInnes

Frankie Love took up his career as a ponce about the same time as Edward Justice became vice-squad detective. Except that neither man was particularly suited for his job, all they had in common was an interest in crime. But, as any ponce or copper will tell you, appearances are not always what they seem. Provocative and honest and acidly funny, *Mr Love and Justice* is the final volume of Colin MacInnes's famous London trilogy.

An Ice-Cream War   William Boyd

As millions are slaughtered on the Western Front, a ridiculous and little-reported campaign is being waged in East Africa – a war they continued after the Armistice because no one told them to stop. 'A towering achievement' – John Carey, Chairman of the Judges of the 1982 Booker Prize, for which this novel was shortlisted.

Every Day is Mother's Day   Hilary Mantel

An outrageous story of lust, adultery, madness, death and the social services. 'Strange . . . rather mad . . . extremely funny . . . she sometimes reminded me of the early Muriel Spark' – Auberon Waugh

1982 Janine   Alasdair Gray

Set inside the head of an ageing, divorced, alcoholic, insomniac supervisor of security installations who is tippling in the bedroom of a small Scottish hotel – this is a most brilliant and controversial novel.

A CHOICE OF PENGUIN FICTION

A Fanatic Heart Edna O'Brien

'A selection of twenty-nine stories (including four new ones) full of wit and feeling and savagery that prove that Edna O'Brien is one of the subtlest and most lavishly gifted writers we have' – A. Alvarez in the *Observer*

Charade John Mortimer

'Wonderful comedy . . . an almost Firbankian melancholy . . . John Mortimer's hero is helplessly English' – *Punch*. 'What is *Charade*? Comedy? Tragedy? Mystery? It is all three and more' – *Daily Express*

Casualties Lynne Reid Banks

'The plot grips; the prose is fast-moving and elegant; above all, the characters are wincingly, winningly human . . . if literary prizes were awarded for craftsmanship and emotional directness, *Casualties* would head the field' – *Daily Telegraph*

The Anatomy Lesson Philip Roth

The hilarious story of Nathan Zuckerman, the famous forty-year-old writer who decides to give it all up and become a doctor – and a pornographer – instead. 'The finest, boldest and funniest piece of fiction which Philip Roth has yet produced' – *Spectator*

Gabriel's Lament Paul Bailey

Shortlisted for the 1986 Booker Prize
'The best novel yet by one of the most careful fiction craftsmen of his generation' – *Guardian*. 'A magnificent novel, moving, eccentric and unforgettable. He has a rare feeling for language and an understanding of character which few can rival' – *Daily Telegraph*

Small Changes Marge Piercy

In the Sixties the world seemed to be making big changes – but for many women it was the small changes that were the hardest and the most profound. *Small Changes* is Marge Piercy's explosive new novel about women fighting to make their way in a man's world.